.ER EDUCATION

Edward Buscombe
SERIES EDITOR

Colin MacCabe and David Meeker
SERIES CONSULTANTS

Cinema is a fragile medium. Many of the great classic films of the past now exist, if at all, in damaged or incomplete prints. Concerned about the deterioration in the physical state of our film heritage, the National Film and Television Archive, a Division of the British Film Institute, has compiled a list of 360 key films in the history of the cinema. The long-term goal of the Archive is to build a collection of perfect showprints of these films, which will then be screened regularly at the Museum of the Moving Image in London in a year-round repertory.

BFI Film Classics is a series of books commissioned to stand alongside these titles. Authors, including film critics and scholars, film-makers, novelists, historians and those distinguished in the arts, have been invited to write on a film of their choice, drawn from the Archive's list. Each volume presents the author's own insights into the chosen film, together with a brief production history and a detailed filmography, notes and bibliography. The numerous illustrations have been specially made from the Archive's own prints.

With new titles published each year, the BFI Film Classics series will rapidly grow into an authoritative and highly readable guide to the great films of world cinema.

Could scarcely be improved upon ... informative, intelligent, jargon-free companions.
The Observer

Cannily but elegantly packaged BFI Classics will make for a neat addition to the most discerning shelves.
New Statesman & Society

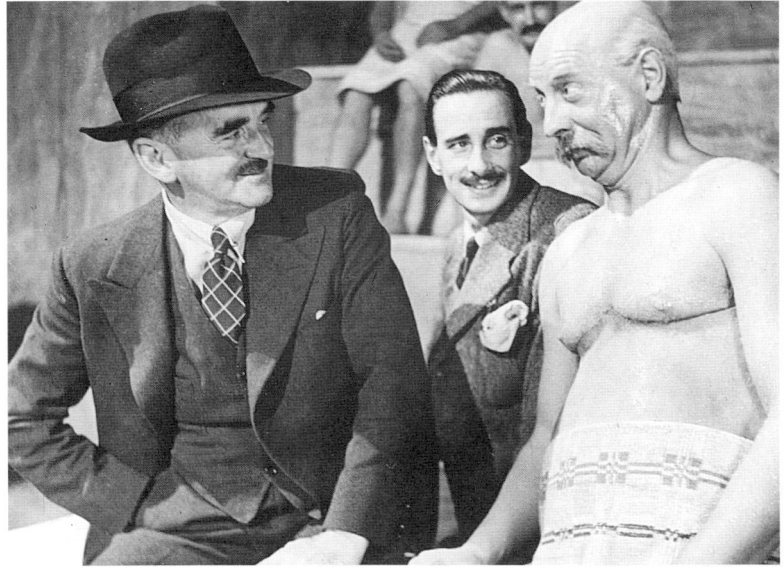

Roger Livesey with make-up artist George Blackler (centre) and David Low (left), cartoonist and creator of Colonel Blimp

THE LIFE AND DEATH
OF COLONEL BLIMP

. . . .

A. L. Kennedy

BRITISH FILM INSTITUTE

bfi

BFI PUBLISHING

First published in 1997 by the
BRITISH FILM INSTITUTE
21 Stephen Street, London W1P 2LN

Copyright © A. L. Kennedy 1997

The British Film Institute exists
to promote appreciation, enjoyment, protection and
development of moving image culture in and throughout the
whole of the United Kingdom.
Its activities include the National Film and
Television Archive; the National Film Theatre;
the Museum of the Moving Image;
the London Film Festival; the production and
distribution of film and video; funding and support for
regional activities; Library and Information Services;
Stills, Posters and Designs; Research;
Publishing and Education; and the monthly
Sight and Sound magazine.

British Library Cataloguing-in-Publication Data
A catalogue record for this book is available from the British Library

ISBN 0–85170–568–5

Designed by
Andrew Barron & Collis Clements Associates

Typesetting by
D R Bungay Associates, Burghfield, Berks.

Printed in Great Britain

CONTENTS

ACKNOWLEDGMENTS

I am particularly indebted to Kevin Macdonald for his humane and lovely biography of Emeric Pressburger and to Faber's excellent edition of the script of *The Life and Death of Colonel Blimp*, edited by Ian Christie.

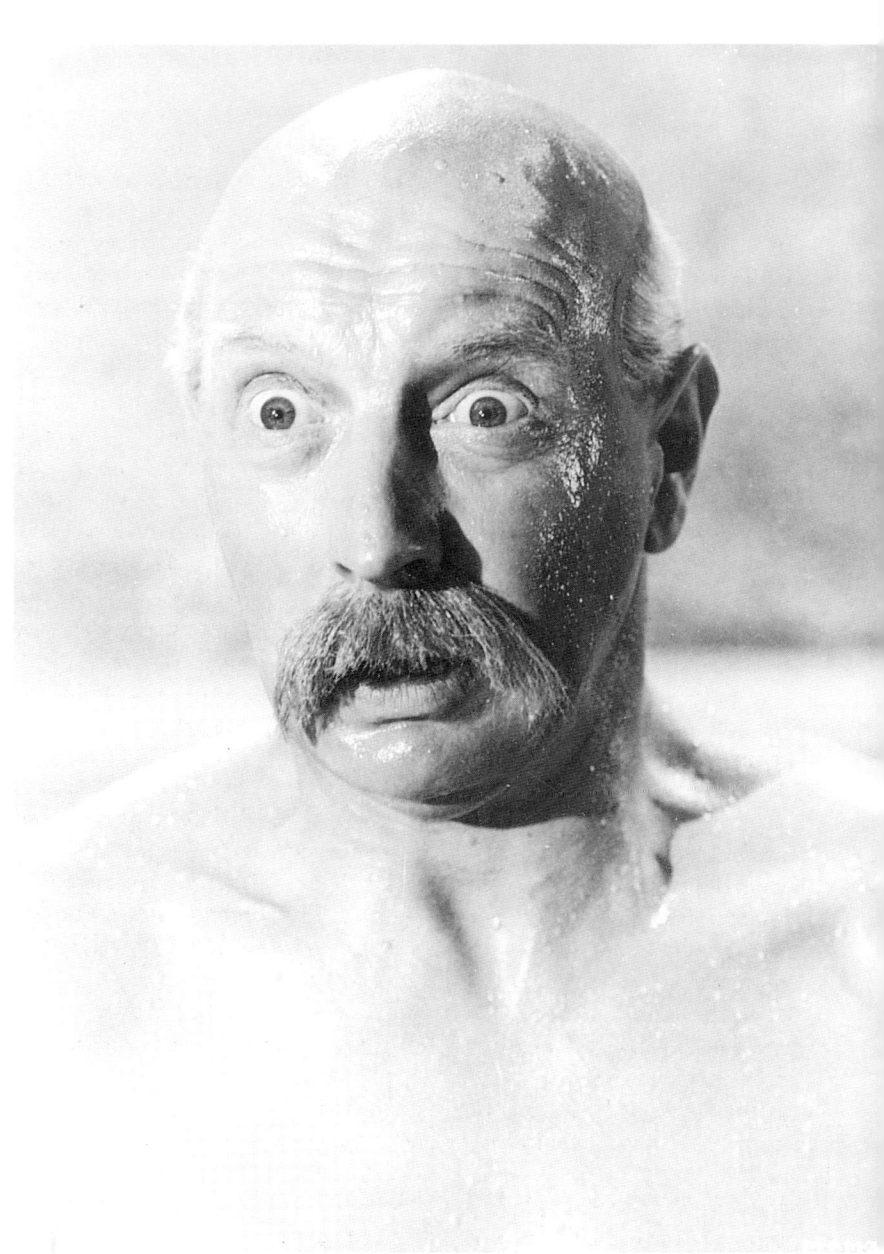

8   Clive Candy confronted by 'Spud'

SOHO AND HOME
. . . .

'... how many times have I told you that a film is not words ... it is thoughts, and feelings, surprises, suspense, accident.'

Emeric Pressburger to Michael Powell[1]

In London, in Soho, in the early spring of 1996, I am walking down from Chinatown to the underground at Leicester Square and I am cold, very cold, and something catches in my mind: the inarticulate punch of somewhere I can only summarise as home. I am thinking of home.

I am a northeastern Scot and I am walking through a yapping northeastern wind that happily sharpens itself between buildings and spits narrow snow in my eyes. And this is how it always felt, the wind at home. It numbed the mouth and then the face, but reamed out the sinuses with splendidly cracking pain. It distorted vision, rounded shoulders, slowed uncomfortable time to a black-iced stop, and even twenty years later it can wrench me back to a place where I want chicken risotto for dinner because it's Wednesday and then an empty evening, not thinking of school, and then sleep under one particular purple quilt while the big outside stays outside, but shudders at the window frames.

My forehead hurts so much that I want to cry, but I might be inclined to in any case. A person is supposed to cry when unexpectedly struck by thoughts of home.

Scots, even today, tend not to dress appropriately against cold – they thole it instead. They wince in its face and dare it to be more miserable than sin and it obliges. When I grew up in Dundee, when I went out to school in the winter in the dark and then came home again in another dark, I tholed it. I wore a school uniform composed of duffle felt and draughts and I tholed that, too. From October to May, I had a headache and persistently lost gloves and I tholed it all.

In Soho, in London, I hear myself remembering Scotland with another Scot. We exchange little myths and clichés; emotional composites standing in place of facts, because these are what make a proper sense of home and we are talking about our home. If we did not do this, we might feel lonely or undefined.

I'm afraid a good deal of my childhood and my home will shuffle through this book for a variety of reasons. This stems partly from the accidents attending my acquaintance with the work of Emeric Pressburger and Michael Powell and partly from the particular themes of *The Life and Death of Colonel Blimp.*

I will immediately point out that these themes have fascinated me since childhood and ran through my early years like continuing friendships. They form part of my comprehension of my self, my personal truth, my understanding of life and death, of time and home. If home is where the heart is, they are very much my home.

And what are these themes? They are comprehension of self, personal truth, understanding of life and death, time and home. Do they fascinate me because they were in at the start of me; or were they so strong, so early because I was born to be so fascinated by them? Undoubtedly, they will form a circular progress here, from beginning to beginning, childhood to childhood, of which I feel Powell and Pressburger – masters of the circular and elliptical plot – might have approved.

I first met *Colonel Blimp* and the other films of Powell and Pressburger, of their Archers production company, when I was still a child. I misheard their names and (not inappropriately) translated them into one entity – Powallan Pressburger. I loved everything Powallan Pressburger had ever made, accepting each film, much as Winston Churchill might have, as a magical but absolute and influential reality.

I did not understand cinema as a process, as something which might be made, as words which might be written or performed; I simply believed in the truths it made. I understood reality was very rarely best reflected by realism. My experience of reality had taught me that it was far more imaginative, quixotic and emotionally charged than anything to do with facts had a right to be. I was also entirely certain, but could not in any way have explained, that an emotional truth, a psychological honesty, a celebratory respect for a medium and those who collaborate in it (including an audience) will create a fabric which can contain the uncontainable – those parts of us which are most human and most beyond the reach of words.

Powallan Pressburger gave me the ungivable – a genuine sense of home. Because although I was born in the northeast of Scotland, although I can feel nostalgia for it now, I am equally sure it was never entirely home. My parents had arrived there from England, via Australia, and brought me up to speak as they did, using the words they used. This meant that I did not sound like the people I met in my home town, or the children I was educated with at school. I could learn the language – I still have a protective tendency to borrow other people's accents – but it was not the language of my heart and mind. I was a foreigner.

Equally, my mother brought me a strong feeling of identification with her own Welsh inheritance. I had and have a great love for Wales, its people and its language. An oddly high proportion of my friends are Welsh. I clearly remember standing with my schoolfriends at a Wales–Scotland rugby international, the only one cheering for Wales. But of the Welsh and cheering contingent I was probably the only one who had not yet ever been to Wales. I would be a foreigner there, too.

Between the ages of five and fifteen, I was forced to inhabit the 1970s. It is, of course, *de rigueur* to ridicule the period now, but I loathed it even then. It was all beyond tholing. I hated the flares and the platform soles, the disco music, the hideous camp pseudo-Scottishness embodied by the Bay City Rollers and so willingly embraced by so many otherwise sane Scots. I hated the fact that Scotland seemed locked in an age where it had no culture beyond football and kilted fat men with sad kneecaps singing sentimental pap. I was out of time.

Dundee in the 70s was being knocked down to make way for an exciting succession of gap sights and temporary car parks. Our one available holiday postcard showed a sun-bleached picture of the High Street as it had been fifteen years before. First generation middle-class, I had benefited from good feeding in a working-class town where many generations had not. By the time I reached my teens, I was taller than a disturbingly large proportion of Dundonian adults. And I went to the city's public day school – the one with the neo-classical facade, indistinguishable from that of the Utica Insane Asylum – the one that sat plumb in the middle of the city centre behind a wide, complacent playground like an open invitation to revolt. I was culpably out of place.

I am happy to admit that I was born middle-aged, that I was an unathletic, grimly reading child and that I have a temperamental tendency to feel out of joint, but even despite all this my surroundings already made me long to find some kind of genuine home, my personal roots. And roots were there and waiting in the black and white or hypernaturally coloured universe of the films I loved – the *real* films of the 30s, 40s and 50s. I fell in love with the quietly anarchic heroes of

Capra and Korda and the Ealing Studios. I longed for honest men with achingly neat haircuts and trouser turn-ups to set everything right. Jimmy Stewart and Henry Fonda taught me about justice and integrity. I adored the gleeful sleaze and intelligence of Humphrey Bogart and James Mason. I adored the cylindrical head and stately bearing of Mervyn Johns and the animal grace of Cary Grant. I adored Alec Guinness's everything.

And, yes, I do realise that I haven't mentioned any of the women. Googie Withers and her ilk did very little for me, but then again, I didn't want them to. If I needed women to look up to I could idolise Katharine Hepburn and be in awe of Marlene Dietrich. If I actually wanted entertainment and the first incomprehensible twitches of lust, I watched the men. There were lots of men and they dressed and behaved and spoke in exactly the ways that I wanted them to. Whole reels could go by without sight of a woman and the filmic focus of attention was very often sexist and male-centred. Me, too.

And while they beguiled my budding hormones and shaped my tastes, the old movies showed me an open-hearted America and a Britain largely composed of Celtic communities, possessed of immense

1 2   Edith, Theo and Clive in the sanatorium

intelligence and perspective, who could beat the best in London. Britain's capital was still the neat and alien standard of excellence, but there already lurked the possibility that some of us might simply not wish to beat or even acknowledge it. My films showed me people who were important – not necessarily because of what they did or had. They mattered because they were people and people matter. The human face of London they gave me was Lavender Hill and Pimlico and streets almost empty of traffic which froze for one respectful minute every Armistice Day. I am still ridiculously pleased that my publisher's offices are in Vauxhall Bridge Road and that I can walk there through Pimlico, looking for Stanley Holloway and proper policemen with bicycle clips.

Boulting Brothers, London Films, Gainsborough, Ealing, Gaumont British, RKO Radio – those strange and long gone names – I had an almost pathetic affection for every one. Each of them brought me close to home, but no one could take me right to the doorstep the way that Powallan Pressburger could. Pressburger could build all the elements I craved into an almost entirely perfect form. He offered a fundamental belief in humanity that flowered in a depth of characterisation and dialogue and in a forgiveness and understanding that extended even to villains. Which meant, of course, that those villains were believable, while the heroes (and even Googie Withers) could break your heart.

A Powallan Pressburger protagonist was *real*, which is to say that he or she was unreal in a way which was entirely truthful to his or her presentation within a given fiction and within an audience member's imagination. Powallan Pressburger made possible that impossible thing – that a film should happen to a real person. Scooped up inside celluloid worlds, their characters fail and triumph and are deeply, almost palpitatingly alive; sensual in their vulnerability; hypnotising in their passion, joy and pain. They take remarkable action because they are human beings, and human beings are remarkable.

Within those celluloid worlds, film was allowed to be fully itself; articulate beyond any limits other than those of its own nature. Light and colour were manipulated to produce images which could speak as delicately as painting or still photography; which could enunciate subtexts, atmospheres and tones of emotion. Scenery might be wantonly theatrical or apparently factual, but always it would say exactly what it had to, exactly as loudly as it should.

Lay aside the screaming verticals and breathless moments of *Black Narcissus*, which of course was mainly about nuns and very adult sexuality and so didn't interest me too much. Think only of Anton Walbrook as Lermontov standing still in *The Red Shoes*. In a wonderfully slow shot we see a silhouette against the light of a window. Our eyes become accustomed to the detail of a pale shirt, a dark suit; we can grasp the pattern of a man whose face is a mask of exhaled cigarette smoke – a barrier, a fiction, a tangible sigh. It has always hurt, just a little, to watch things so beautiful and so resonant in so many parts of my mind. I've spent years of my life inadvertently and impossibly looking for Lermontov.

I loved to listen to their pictures – I still do. Slipping and tickling across every frame came orchestration of unparalleled articulacy. Their scores could swing from wonderfully appropriate pastiche to the kind of operatic structures which unified their later work and pioneered the idea of scored films. The concept of a film's unbroken melody had always been there in the words and the silences, the humour and the freshness of even the slightest Pressburger script. The colour and pitch of voices weave precise melodies and harmonies; languages mingle, as do their strange blends of personalities.

The Powallan Pressburger process of casting – that peculiar mix of luck, instinct, vision and availability – seemed consistently to uncover the unfamiliar in talents, talents in the unfamiliar. The people in their films could seem an odd bunch; unconventional and even fragile. But they always belonged together, worked together and revealed depth after depth of coherent, human substance. They were also immensely appealing.

Powallan Pressburger loved to present an initial character portrait, fascinating but incomplete, and then to redefine and deepen it, using its own past. No one should ever be taken at face value. Anyone can have hidden qualities, unseen life. In his opening scene in *The Life and Death of Colonel Blimp*, Clive Candy, as his oldest incarnation, shouts: 'You laugh at my big belly, but you don't know how I got it! You laugh at my moustache, but you don't know why I grew it! How do you know what sort of man I was ... forty years ago?'[2] When we return to Candy's present in the final scenes of the film, we will know what sort of man he was and is. Once again, we will have learned what quietly remarkable process it took to make the sum of someone.

Powallan Pressburger led me into the type of familiarity that breeds respect. I grew to love his people, places and things and they brought me home. I was not necessarily made comfortable, but I was certainly entranced, convinced and firmly at home.

Of course, *Colonel Blimp* concerns itself very much with an exhaustive definition and exploration of what a home might be: a time, a building, a country, a marriage, a life, an army, a duty, a youth, a faith, a feeling, a state of mind.

Clive 'Sugar' Candy, the film's hero – but a man only ever shown on the brink of heroism – is never allowed a home. In many ways he lives the life of a child. He is looked after by what often seem entirely arbitrary authorities. What he has seems always to have been provided, or imposed, by others – sometimes according to his wishes and often not. He is trusting, open, unselfconscious and painfully innocent; a man living a *Boy's Own* life, deprived of emotional fulfilment but resounding with pointless activity and want. If he is unaware of his passions, or leaves them largely unspoken, this is because his pains have become habitual, a part of personality, and because he was never taught a language that could speak of emotions like pain.

Spud leading manoeuvres

Pain, now there's a thing – a little path to take us round and start us at the start again. *The Life and Death of Colonel Blimp* makes a part of my childhood and my home, because it formed a relief from and an identification with pain.

In 1978 the BBC screened a season of films by what I finally learned was the writing, production and directing team of Michael Powell and Emeric Pressburger, who were commercially united as The Archers in 1941. Much as I had done with an earlier Ealing Studios retrospective, I now drowned in a mainline supply of my loves. I could go home.

1978 also saw the first year of stillness after my parents' separation. Having quite literally lost my home and then moved a number of my belongings to four different addresses in one year, I started to live what would become my new life with my mother in a flat, very much smaller than what had been the family home. People I loved cried. People I loved were hurt. Money was difficult. At my school and amongst my friends divorce was unusual, turmoil unspeakable and only certain kinds of financial embarrassment acceptable. Suddenly a great deal of what I was and what had happened to me was unmentionable and therefore, in a way, unreal.

Starting war before midnight at Clive's club

Other children have lived through far more unfortunate situations. I am not making any special case for myself, or trying to say that the adults around me did anything other than what they thought would be their best. I know that the parts of my nature which are arrogant, unforgiving, thuggish and desperately fond of privacy did not help my situation. I often felt exposed and under threat, and this made me illtempered. In short, my new life did not agree with me and I felt more of a refugee than ever. I wanted to be Home.

Mr Powell and Mr Pressburger were there for me then and I loved them for it. They brought me friends, the release inherent in beauty, a cleansing access for grief, and a way to approach all the ideas that were ricocheting round my head. Delicately, melodically, thoroughly, they turned in their hands a comprehension of self, personal truth, understanding of life and death, time and home. Emeric Pressburger, scriptwriter, gave me what I needed. Emeric Pressburger, writer of *The Life and Death of Colonel Blimp*, European Jewish refugee, a man who had to build an identity, a working relation with a language and a home in Hungary, then Romania, then Germany, then France and finally Britain, gave me the ungivable. Emeric Pressburger, with *Blimp*, helped me to open the place in my heart which would be not a home anywhere, but a *longing* for Home anywhere. He offered me the first signs of a free and wonderful desire for the perfect Home which my life, my thought, my action and my love can always grow towards. He gave me an insatiable ache, but one which is to do with living and creating and not with death.

Perhaps of all the Powell and Pressburger creations, *Blimp* came closest to reaching the unreachable and catching it in the spaces between its words. It is almost insanely bent upon dealing with the most delicate, intangible and subjective elements of time and character. This is a film about loss and longing, about creating the impossible and then setting it beyond your grasp. This is a film about home and the meaning of home, the meaning of self. This is a film which lies in the most human ways but tells remarkable, human truths. Here, to quote from Lermontov in *The Red Shoes*, 'Time passes by, love passes by, life passes by', in a way which is more poignant and savagely forgiving, more melancholy, troubling and revealing, than almost any other cinematic work I have encountered.

The Life and Death of Colonel Blimp is a deeply personal piece, which allows me the dignity and privilege of a personal response.

Those of you without copies of the script or – even better – the video of *The Life and Death of Colonel Blimp* might be well advised to beg, steal, hire, buy or borrow them at this point. Everyone should have them anyway, but they will certainly help you here. When I respond personally I am never at my most coherent and, even if I were, the film is its own best companion and critique. In its inception, its creation and its final form it is, as Mr Pressburger knew, not only words, but thoughts and feelings, surprises, suspense, accident.

A LOVE OF FLAGS

'The over complication of ideas is much more dangerous.'
From Ministry of Information report on version of script for *The Life and Death of Colonel Blimp.*[3]

Sentimental, even plaintive music plays while we let the camera rove us idly over a quaint, embroidered tapestry from (perhaps) an English country house. The figures portrayed – particularly that of Blimp on horseback – are unrealistic, stylised, stiff and touched with both the nobility of knighthood and the foolishness of Don Quixote.

Now we move suddenly to the south-east of England, 1942. Titles over, *The Life and Death of Colonel Blimp* begins.

Shown in the curious peach-blushed, high Jack Cardiff colour of an Archers' team production, we see a form being laboriously typed out. Whether this is a tedious requisition or a coded signal is not entirely clear. Next – solemn, purposeful, almost ludicrous – a massed wing of motorcycle messengers batters through docile, livid-green countryside, riders gradually peeling off for their various destinations. American-style swing music beats out while our pace continues to drive forward.

A lone despatch rider is cheerfully ambushed by his own side as he approaches 'B' Company field HQ. After a brusque, faintly racist, faintly sexist, faintly fascist dialogue between Lieutenant 'Spud' Wilson and his jolly company, we are off to see and then arrest Clive Candy, 'The Wizard'. The army's signal has been delivered and then reinterpreted.

'B' Company is to take part in Exercise Beer Mug against the Home Guard. War starts at midnight. But Spud and his men mean to steal a march on the Home Guard and begin the war hours beforehand; thus negating the whole purpose and value of the exercise and disobeying the chain of command.

Spud makes a brief diversion to meet a girl in the ATS. We don't quite know why. In a scene we don't see, she knocks him ignominiously unconscious and drives off to warn Major-General Clive Candy and the rest of the Home Guard command. Spud is discovered, flat on his back.

'B' Company thunder away in heated pursuit of the ATS girl. The big band reasserts its claims on the score while we settle in our seats, partly excited by the speed and energy of the action, partly revolted by its dreadfully everyday, mindless threat. We are seeing a small picture of war. Here is the excitement of training as it swings into gear effectively, the buzz of power, of youth, of certainty and mob consciousness. Here is the love of one's fellows and their reinforcement of one's qualities or one's prejudices and faults. Here is combat as sport, as daring and as revenge for an unexpected bump on the head. We are not being shown a simple manifesto for or against war, or a type of war. We are being offered war's portrait. We do see the opinion of the painters – about which, more later – but during the course of the script we also see a deep and rounded representation of the subject.

The opening of *Blimp* never fails to shock me. To genuinely shock me. A maniac in a ski mask doesn't leap from a cupboard and knife a pregnant woman in the throat – we are not dealing here with a cheap assault on my nervous system. This is a film which from the very outset will tease out my beliefs and test them to their limits. My neat assumptions and Achilles' heels can all be caught up and dissected in the complex network of realities and conflicts which Powell and Pressburger set out. Ideas here will be complicated – one with another – because that is the nature of ideas. I can only really begin to understand that nature when I see ideas set in relation to each other and to the human beings, time and culture which hold them.

By this I don't mean that the film will be foggy, unpleasant, or hard to enjoy. Even its meaning – something allegedly notoriously hard to pin down – will be, in all the most important ways, plain to an observer. It will simply be difficult to explain *Blimp* without simply repeating it word for word and then including all it adds above and between. This means that critics and reviewers and men from the MoI will find it infuriating and professionally inexplicable. But a viewer can simply experience *Blimp*'s totality; can let its subliminal, overt and interactive elements do their work, and can also enjoy a remarkable love story which deals with two remarkable loves – Clive Candy's repeating obsession with Edith Hunter and each of the central characters' longings for a worthy home.

Blimp is complex without being complicated. Any audience member's response can be equally complex and mine is no exception. At many levels I have very good reasons to hate this film, but I do not. Before I return to *Blimp*'s exploration of war, its conduct and conductors, I will mention a few of these reasons, a few of the factors, governing my response.

Seeking to nourish my mind and sensibilities, my parents would often take me on vaguely indigestible rambles through art galleries, museums, stately homes and churches. I have great difficulty understanding purely visual information and found the galleries hot and tiring – they left me with a feeling of incurable stupidity. Museums were more palatable; they had clearer connections with people. But, like many children, I craved the excitement of clear and preferably violent purpose in objects. I was drawn to arms and armour, to the filigree and inlay that once graced the instruments of organised slaughter.

I was (tentatively) a Scot and had gone to a Scottish school. This meant that I had almost no grasp of my country's history and culture beyond a drab list of early saints and the cultivation of oats by the run-rig system. The faint smell of blood and struggle about old blades was really the only tangible link I could sense with my past. My Welsh roots were even more fragile, consisting of a language my great-grandmother had chosen not to pass on and surreal stories of charabanc rides and alcoholic trance states which made Dylan Thomas – when I came to read him – very much like an honorary uncle.

I was propelled through many of Scotland's many country houses and hypnotised by the vast fans and rosettes of muskets, swords and targes which bloomed in every stairwell and hall. Arranged by minds similar to those which titivate catacombs with snugly crossed thighbones and pyramids of balanced skulls, these hordes of weaponry gave me the impression that an ancient, amalgamated army still lingered somewhere, waiting for its chance.

Above all, I fell in love with the flags. Every sacred building of any size had its battery of flags, worn to reddened gossamer by time. Alma,

Sebastopol, Lucknow, Ypres, Dunkirk – the gold-embroidered names rang with a note I could not recognise but which was undoubtedly uplifting. I would walk under high vaults in dusty light and imagine each standard, looking out across its battlefield, rippling above the bodies of men who were willing to die for it. I had been told about this phenomenon and seen it portrayed in films – men would die to protect the substance of these flags.

The connection between flags and countries, armies, or even regiments, was something I never made. I was also unaware that centuries of cultural oppression and manipulation, along with campaigns of militarisation and armed occupation, had made it very likely that I would connect feelings of Scottishness almost solely with military display. Until very recently Scottish national dress was only presented in the form imposed upon highland dress by the necessities of the English/ British army. The endless migraine of tartans presented to me as the bulk of my cultural heritage was largely an equally spurious invention, created for the benefit of non-Scots. My childhood's quintessence of Scottish identity in the 70s seemed to be made up largely of uniforms, tartans (the Kennedy has a large yellow streak), arms, armour, martial bands and music, with the occasional relief of a (proud but defeated) football strip. When I was dressed in my nice white blouse and my white knee socks, black T-bar Clarks shoes and Royal Stewart kilt, I am quite sure that I looked like a little girl. But I felt like *a Soldier, a Scottish Soldier, who wandered far away ...*

To be Scottish was to fight the English and to lose. To be Welsh was to fight the English and to lose. To love and to die for a flag, there was no other way.

It took a good while for me to connect the idea of loving and dying and flags to the idea of war. And I do mean the *idea* of war, rather than its fact.

Most of my relatives of an age to have served in the Second World War were in reserved occupations. The stories I grew up with from that period were of happy activities in the black market and anarchic camaraderie. Only my Great Uncle Cyril went away to fight. I have a small black-and-white picture of him, handsome in a new uniform and forage cap, leaning on an army truck. He was captured by the Japanese and made to work on the Burma Railway. This, I am told, sent him slightly mad for a while.

I've met him since but what I seem to remember of him is a tall, thin man who moved gently and without sound and came to me once in his garden and gave me fresh strawberries, still warm from the sun. Strawberries I could eat right then, not waiting for a meal time. Strawberries that hadn't been washed; shining, pampered fruit that came from an English garden and not a dusty Scottish berry field. I can't recall him speaking to me, but I know we were both in agreement that I would enjoy the fruit and should eat them before anybody found us and objected. The idea of impromptu food seemed always to upset my significant adults.

Great Uncle Cyril had been in a war and it had made him different. I could imagine him going out to a place where pain and death could touch him, making that terrible sacrifice and letting it change him. I could not imagine Great Uncle Cyril killing anyone.

Killing – that was the part of war and soldiering I hadn't considered. I could watch Alec Guinness fly off into black-and-white skies above Malta, never to return, and this was sad but made a kind of sense. Alec Guinness strafing refugees to death or flame-throwing into pillboxes until they sizzled with the faintly bacon smell of roasted flesh – that seemed far less comprehensible.

My filmic education had taught me respect for the generation which not only won the last war, but also fought for massive social changes before and after peace. John Doe and George Bailey didn't go to war – they fought campaigns of a quietly vicious, domestic kind. For these men, even moderate violence seemed cataclysmic – as, indeed, it is. If my movie friends did finally fight, their actions were governed by decency and a desire to defend the dear and the right. The combatant's lot was one of sad necessity, underlined by a moral ambiguity. Beyond the more trashy propaganda efforts, my films showed the high command as distant and ill-informed while the men and women in less ornamented uniform risked their lives. All had to embrace the destructive imperatives of warfare, and those imperatives were a two-edged sword. I was taught that killing changed people for the worse and, ultimately, took second place to the struggles and changes among civilians at home. I was slowly becoming an instinctive pacifist.

Nevertheless, walking through the apparently bombed city centre of 70s Dundee, I could feel assured that – at one time – a generation had existed who could create new worlds out of rubble, a generation so

Clive, newly decorated with the VC, with 'Period Blimp' (centre) and 'Hoppy'

Clive at the War Office

precious it was willing to be sacrificed. My city, ill-used for centuries by self-interested oligarchies, had been physically wrecked by greed and stupidity, decades after the war.

I have since met and talked with a great many people of the war generation and I do find them to have been and to still be remarkable people. Women who drove trams through bombing and lifted live land mines off roofs without thinking. Men who ran across foreign beaches while the air and the earth exploded all about them and who knew their survival then did not depend on fitness, or training, or their worth as human beings, but on an insane kind of chance. These were people who broke ranks to try to comfort concentration camp survivors being loaded on refugee ships, afraid of where they might next be sent. These were ordinary people suddenly swept up in events on a cinematic scale, who tried to respond with their best. These were people like my grandmother. She would tell me, still angry after so many years, of watching men march away to the 1914–18 war and seeing none of them return. She had watched them march again, to the next war, and felt betrayed.

I love and respect my grandmother's generation and I love and respect what I see of them in *Blimp*. But of course this film does not only deal with what is lovely and deserving of respect. *Blimp* faces some of the greatest evils humanity can contemplate.

When Spud Wilson breaks into Candy's club in St James's, he bawls triumphantly, 'Brute force and ruddy ignorance!' He then leads a group of armed and uniformed young men into a Turkish bath full of elderly, bemused gentlemen, dressed only in towels. The camera tracks straight through walls, keeping pace with Spud as he batters deeper and deeper into the rooms of the painstakingly lavish Denham set – more than fifty feet long – and rifles are turned on frail bodies. The scene is at once ridiculous and savage. Although Pressburger, whose mother was murdered in Auschwitz, could not have known this at the time, today the invasion of the baths may also remind us of photographs from the holocaust. The uniforms are different, the half-naked bodies are better fed, less immediately threatened, but an edge of surreal horror remains.

Finally Spud reaches a recumbent figure – fat, bald, lobster-red and sweating. This is Major-General Clive Wynne-Candy and he will never be more of a Blimp than he is now. Neither man seems likely to win our hearts as a protagonist. Spud hectors and bullies while Candy stands on his purloined dignity. Until this point Spud's energy and ingenuity may have won the day. He certainly represents a future of speed and efficiency. He can calmly summarise war – *the real thing* – as 'our losses divided by ten and the enemy's multiplied by twenty!'[4]

The original version of this line may give us a clearer idea of why this script is not simply a mindless endorsement of Total War. Pressburger intended the dialogue to run:

> SPUD: And tell them to make it like the real thing.
> STUFFY: What do they mean by 'like the real thing', Spud?
> SPUD: (*Savagely*) Well, obviously, prisoners must be bayoneted to death, women must be raped, our losses divided by ten and the enemy's multiplied by twenty!
> STUFFY: Yessir.[5]

Spud is happy to beat the Nazis by becoming one. He is not merely advocating a new efficiency, he is destroying morality. Spud would unhinge the home he is fighting for in order to save it, or – more accurately – his little world of 'B' Company and himself.

In terms of the emotional storyline Spud is finally too unsympathetic for his own good when he insults and underestimates Candy and is – once again – humiliated by a supposed physical inferior when Candy throws him into the bath. This is the first time that Candy will be used as a yardstick to judge the value of other characters. Those who dismiss him and cannot see his qualities – usually men from one ministry or another – are set beyond the pale. They are, in the spirit of David Low's cartoons, truly Blimps.

But before he plunges into the waters of an extended flashback with Candy, the profusely sweating Spud articulates what has always been proposed as *Blimp*'s central message. Using the exercise as a metaphor for Britain's (or more precisely England's) conduct of the war, he advocates a new spirit of enterprise.

> SPUD: You say, 'War starts at midnight' – how do you know the enemy says so, too?
> CANDY: (*Stares; then quite mildly*) But my dear fellow, that was agreed, wasn't it?
> SPUD: (*By now the sweat is streaming off him from heat and fury*) Agreed – my foot! How many agreements have been kept by the

> enemy since this War started? We agree to the rules of the game
> and they keep kicking us in the seat of the pants. When I joined
> the army, the only agreement I entered into was to defend my
> country by any means at my disposal, not by National Sporting
> Club Rules but by every means that has existed since Cain
> slugged Abel![6]

Spud is not a man who is willing to die for a flag; he is willing to kill for
himself. As an individual point of view this does make a kind of immoral
sense. A wider application of his beliefs would, of course, bring the
home he is creating close to military dictatorship.

In a memorandum to the Films Division of the Ministry of
Information Powell and Pressburger reply to the Ministry's criticisms of
Blimp's draft script. Point number three reads:

> We are challenged to state clearly the ideas towards which the
> audiences are to be directed.
>
> What are the chief qualities of Clive Candy? They are the
> qualities of the average Englishman: an anxiety to believe the best
> of other people: Fairness in fighting, based upon games: Fairness
> after the fight is over: a natural naiveté engendered by class,
> insularity and the permeability of the English language.
>
> We think these are splendid virtues: so splendid that, in
> order to preserve them, it is worthwhile shelving them until we
> have won the war.[7]

It is important to remember that this document is fighting to win support
for a film. The Archers had something to say and wanted to be able to say
it; they wanted the government's moral (and hopefully financial)
support, something almost indispensable in a wartime production; and
they wanted to persuade the Admiralty that their project was worthy
enough for them to release Laurence Olivier from service to star as Clive
Candy. This means that Powell and Pressburger may not have been
lying, but may very well have been gearing what they said to please a
very specific readership.

I am convinced that Powell and Pressburger wanted to assist the
war effort. Pressburger had seen Nazism and anti-Semitism face to face
in Berlin before the war. If Britain lost the war he must have understood

that he would either be lucky and escape, perhaps to America, or be liquidated. In 1942 – the year of the memorandum – he received a brief Red Cross message from his mother, still in Nazi-occupied Hungary. He would never hear from her again.

I am equally convinced that Pressburger – a gentle, complex and intelligent man – sought to use this most personal of his films to challenge, question and slowly distil the essence of what his adopted country was fighting for and how it was best to fight.

From The Archers' letters to Wendy Hiller (who was to play Edith) and their correspondence with Olivier, we can see that Powell and Pressburger felt themselves to be artistically at their most assured and free. They felt they could do anything and had the right to try. Arthur Rank, who was paying their bills, agreed.

We also know that David Low, the creator of the virulently and accurately satirical Colonel Blimp cartoon character, gave the Archers' script his wholehearted support. I can only guess at why Powell and Pressburger chose Low's character as the focus for a film. Having made that choice, they then ensured that their protagonist – although sometimes Blimpish – never actually attained the rank of Colonel, or the kind of

Edith and Clive, overhearing anti-British propaganda in Berlin

moral death that true Blimp status would demand. Clive Candy could be described as a Trojan horse, innocently bringing humanity into the Blimp heartland. Even the lightning-witted MoI must have been uneasy before they saw the script for a film which claimed to defend their Home by celebrating an anti-establishment icon. *Blimp* never realistically promised to be anything but controversial.

Their letters bear witness to a quietly massive desire to lash out against all Blimps – the ignorant, the xenophobic, the small-minded, the inefficient, the bureaucratic, the established, the powerful and the deadly Blimps. These were in fact just the attributes displayed by the MoI, who objected, for example, to an ironic comment in the film that duelling scars were believed to make Germans more respected by natives of Africa. This, they felt, might show unscarred British colonials in a poor light before the British public. Something else to unnerve the corridors of Whitehall.

I believe that Powell and particularly Pressburger *did* dedicate this film – as they wrote – 'to the New Army of Britain, to the new spirit in warfare, to the new toughness in battle, and to men and women who know what they are fighting for and are fighting this war to win it.'[8] But what exactly is it that those men and women are fighting for? The dedication leaves it noticeably undefined. *Colonel Blimp*, on the other hand, describes what they are fighting for in terms with which the MoI could never agree and would probably never understand. *Blimp* catches a moment when Britain had the chance to plan its future for good or ill. Both the best and the worst possible choices are here on display.

This means that I, as an individual born into the Britain the war generation bequeathed me, can love this film. Its own internal contradictions and its conflicts with my own beliefs are part of what I love about it. *Blimp* makes me think.

Blimp deals with a type and class of English person I have been brought up to regard with distrust, or even contempt. The English army and the English way of fighting have always seemed deeply foreign. On the one hand, the blasphemous idea of war as a game, man-killing as sport, seems as incomprehensible as the braying bluster of young Candy when he meets his army chum Hoppy in the Turkish bath flashback scene. Equally, I have never understood the concept of the polite, almost emotionless conduct of war – that a war *could* begin precisely at midnight.

Perhaps because I am a pacifist I abhor attempts to make the public face of war any less terrible than it is. Perhaps as a Celt I cannot understand a passionless conflict – or, even more disturbing, the desire to make a conflict appear to be passionless. And yet, like the 'Period Blimp' who harangues young Clive for his noise-making and then fawns over his 'damn good' VC, I admire courage and commitment. I do not respect the decision to fight, but I can respect the person who has made it. Beyond this, Roger Livesey's sympathetic portrayal of Candy makes me respect an individual – an individual who has, as usual, been underestimated.

Blimp deals with propaganda and counter-propaganda. Edith and Candy tell me that the British did not maltreat or starve the Boers in South Africa, or put them into the world's first concentration camps. Both Spud and Edith suggest that good sportsmanship and fair play constantly hobble the British army abroad. I have the sudden, surreal impression that the British Empire was only created to allow good Englishmen to go abroad and be terribly nice to foreigners.

Of course, from Scottish and world history, I know that bayoneting prisoners, raping women and other frightfully unsportsmanlike behaviour has, now and again, been something of a standard in various branches of the English/British forces, throughout history. I know that Britain's conduct of the war in South Africa was appalling, even when it came to the care of its own personnel. But I do not doubt that Edith and Clive, and even Spud in his own way, all believe in the good sportsmanship of England and Britain. Britain in this context representing a picturesque and useful extension to the basic fact of England. Spud wants to destroy the nation's complacency, but he is too much a part of it to see where its ignorance, cruelty and self-satisfaction lie. And soon we will see a British army officer (from South Africa, the land of shadowy atrocities) threaten German prisoners illegally in a First World War dugout. Candy has questioned them ineffectually and left – he cannot properly imagine that any harm could befall them in his absence, or that interrogations on either side are ever anything other than gentlemanly. Fair play achieves nothing, but foul play makes us ugly, foreign to ourselves. Only a foreigner, a European, a German like Theo, can show us a way beyond an unhealthy innocence of our blacker motives and towards a genuine good.

Clive is a good and sportsmanlike soldier. I do not believe he could have performed or witnessed atrocities, but he is innocent to the point of stupidity. As he tries to set off for Berlin to aid Edith in her crusade to

cleanse the British reputation abroad – probably by being terribly nice to foreigners – Powell and Pressburger surround Candy with governmental Blimps (who never actually deny the German propaganda). Lost in the consequent maze of diplomatic niceties and doublespeak, he blunders a middling way through Berlin, between ranting German automata and slightly sinister Men from the Embassy, between magnificently polished and helmeted German Uhlans and magnificently polished and helmeted British Guards: haughty, stilted, overdressed and almost indistinguishable. We are being given a glimpse of how the world is really run: with interchangeable troops at the beck and call of unpleasant and unworthy diplomats.

By the time Clive Candy faces Theo Kretschmar-Schuldorff on a duelling piste, I know that he is a terribly deadly kind of child, loose in a dreadful world. He is as far away from home as we will see him travel and yet his nature and the moral conflicts whirling about him mean he is bringing me closer and closer to Home.

MANIFESTO

. . . .

'I must, first of all, because we still don't know one another well, reaffirm our responsibility as independent film-makers.'

Emeric Pressburger in a letter to Wendy Hiller[9]

We have now reached the point where my personal and professional Homes converge. With *Blimp*, Powell and Pressburger have led me forward into a personal exploration of my faith in peace and my expectations of war. They have given me a form of English nationalism I cannot accept as even faintly credible and yet which I can find as beguiling as Theo Kretschmar-Schuldorff (and possibly Emeric Pressburger) did. They show me the boorishness, ignorance and destruction I know cannot be Home – the English establishment I know cannot make my Home – and yet they also conjure up tantalising flickers of what might be.

To someone who might half seriously call herself a professional writer Powell and Pressburger also offer a fascinating pattern for the conduct of what I could term my business and artistic affairs. For *Blimp*, Pressburger mounted his soapbox and presented Wendy Hiller – and the world – with the Archers' manifesto of film-making, a document which

I believe could be easily applied to almost any other creative medium. Had its philosophy been able to flourish in Britain beyond the golden years of The Archers' productions we might, in my underinformed opinion, not have wasted decades with the near-death experience of the British film industry.

Before I begin to rant, I will reproduce the five, lovely points made by Pressburger to Hiller in his attempt to persuade her to play Edith in *Blimp*. These five points do indeed reaffirm the responsibilities of independent film-makers, to say nothing of the confidence of live creativity in one of those rare moments when it manages to recognise its strengths without also indulging its weaknesses.

One, we owe allegiance to nobody except the financial interests which provide our money; and, to them, the sole responsibility of ensuring them a profit, not a loss.

Two, every single foot in our films is our own responsibility and nobody else's. We refuse to be guided or coerced by any influence but our own judgement.

Three, when we start work on a new idea we must be a year ahead, not only of our competitors, but also of the times. A real film, from idea to universal release, takes a year. Or more.

Four, no artist believes in escapism. And we secretly believe that no audience does. We have proved, at any rate, that they will pay to see the truth, for other reasons than her nakedness.

Five, at any time, and particularly at the present, the self-respect of all collaborators, from star to prop-man, is sustained, or diminished, by the theme and purpose of the film they are working on. They will fight or intrigue to work on a subject they feel is urgent or contemporary, and fight equally hard to avoid working on a trivial or pointless subject. And we agree with them and want the best workmen with us; and get them. These are the main things we believe in. They have brought us an unbroken record of success and a unique position. Without the one, of course, we should not enjoy the other very long. We are under no illusions. We know we are surrounded by hungry sharks. But you have no idea what fun it is surf-bathing, if you have only paddled, with a nurse holding on to the back of your rompers. We hope you will come on in, the water's fine.[9]

Wonderful, isn't it? Assured, sensible, enthusiastic and businesslike. This is the voice of someone who wants to be treated with decency and probably will be. This is also the voice of a writer, and I am, of course, always on the side of the writer. To be sure, the Powell and Pressburger films would never have happened without Powell – his drive, his vision and energy were vital. But they wouldn't have happened without Pressburger, either. Pressburger, the man who was often expunged from his own filmography during the 70s, who was reported as dead in 1978 (nine years early) and who received almost no mention when Powell and Pressburger's films were given a BAFTA retrospective. Pressburger the underdog, Pressburger the writer.

Temperamentally, he was not unlikely to go unnoticed. He was small and habitually, but quietly, well-dressed. Like many writers he could be conscientiously invisible, careful not to cloud whatever text he was moving through. He had a confidence in his own abilities that seemed to make him feel it was unnecessary for him to be in any way intrusive in other areas. But he also had a lack of ego which made him an ideal conduit for inspiration and an ideal collaborator – his devotion was to the idea, not to his part in its creation. This could also mean he was,

3 4   Theo recuperating with Edith

like Clive Candy, undervalued or overlooked. Pressburger's early experiences in film at Ufa in Germany echo my own in literature – nervous confusion, followed by the dawning of a small light.

> I was very young, very shy and utterly inexperienced. However, on the first day when I began working with the Stapenhorst group, I felt my shyness fade. I was asked my opinion and what I said was (to my surprise) given serious consideration. All of a sudden I was not only 'present' but – for the first time in my life – recognized as part of the team.[11]

Working with producer Gunther von Stapenhorst, Pressburger's quietness did not mean he was taken for granted. He was given respect as a human being and then offered the space and support to earn further respect through his work. From then on, until the Nazi hold on Germany's culture began to strangle it, Pressburger's work at Ufa flourished.

In *Blimp*, Pressburger takes his refugee past, his European and Jewish alien's conception of Britain and his hopes for its future and draws

Clive fails to say what he means

upon them all. He reflects upon his oddly matched but oddly successful partnership and friendship with Michael Powell – a securely English man who could turn his back on England's culture, a man who could bluster and dazzle a committee meeting before Pressburger slipped in a polite, reasonable, almost by-the-by request for this or that sum. Ultimately their relations broke down, and the team of remarkable professionals The Archers had gathered around them fragmented – partly because of almost inevitable financial and artistic changes, partly because of the darker side of Powell's nature. But in *Blimp* there is the sense of a happy and productive tension being captured. Pressburger's grandson records him as saying that Powell 'knows what I am going to say even before I say it – maybe even before I have thought it – and that is very rare. You are lucky if you meet someone like that once in your life.'[12]

In the script and the manifesto there is also a celebration of the points Pressburger summarises. Both the script and the manifesto give me the pleasure of joining a fine mind to share in its professional and personal experience.

> One, we owe allegiance to nobody except the financial interests which provide our money; and, to them, the sole responsibility of ensuring them a profit, not a loss.

Well, it has to be said, doesn't it? If somebody pays you to produce, you should try to produce something for them that will pay. Fair's fair. I write middling literary fiction – a genre not noted for its fabulous earning powers – but even I have to admit that it is better for a book if it actually earns its advance. Art for Art's sake might work once, but probably no one will bet on it again.

So what am I advocating? What is Pressburger advocating? Why do I read that sentence and feel a tiny flare of joy? Have I always been a Thatcherite at heart?

No. No, I have not.

And, as I'm sure you'd worked out, because you can read just as well as I, Pressburger is talking about rendering unto Caesar what is Caesar's and keeping him the hell away from anything his dreadful paws would ruin beyond all hope of repair. He is establishing a principle which is the exact reverse of that currently in operation in much of our film and television production. Yes, our work must make money, or we and our supporters will go out of business – that is only common sense. We must make decisions that allow us to recoup our expenditures and, apart from anything else, if we don't this may well be an indication that we didn't communicate with our audience as we should have. They didn't understand us, so we have failed.

But beyond this financial bottom line, which is itself already coloured with a creative agenda, our producers/supporters/backers/ angels/publishers *should have no say*. Quality work cannot be produced if the hindmost, grubbiest hair on the terminally dislocated tail is being allowed to wag the dog. Fear of making an incorrect decision (from which grows the inability to make decisions at all) cannot encourage good work. Randomly picking a format, a previously winning formula, a commercial idea, does not guarantee a winning formula now, or a commercial success. What worked before will not – by definition – work as well again. Your audience has already seen it.

Equally, asking your audience what it wants may well be counter-productive. Good work will offer your audience what it didn't know it wanted, what it could never have predicted, what will surprise and entertain and enlarge its expectations. Your audience deserves no less. Playing safe is not safe, it is just terribly tedious and degrading for all concerned. Look at British television if you don't believe me. Or, on second thoughts, don't – poking yourself in the eye with a hot fork would probably be preferable and you don't need a licence for that.

All Pressburger asks is that creative professionals should be allowed to be creative professionally. Would you call in plumbers and then decide what you actually wanted from them was a spot of reroofing, or would the neighbours think more of you if you built a wrought-iron model of Maes Howe to replace your patio? No. But artistic Caesars do roughly that every day in their respective media.

> Two, every single foot in our films is our own responsibility and nobody else's. We refuse to be guided or coerced by any influence but our own judgement.

Yes, yes, yes. Because, within a creative project, no one understands what's going on quite as well as those people who are making it go on. And until the piece is finished it will not – quite naturally – be articulate enough to explain itself.

Now perhaps there is a tiny amount of arrogance at work here, but only a tiny amount. I think it is justifiable for the practitioner of any craft to be allowed to practise that craft to the best of their ability. A writer will usually know the best way to write something, just as a director will probably know how best to direct it. Left to their own devices, they will produce to their limit, because self-improvement is all part of the process. If they fail, they will face the consequences. If they are never given the opportunity to fail, they will also be denied the opportunity to succeed.

Here I will also note that, although *Blimp* was made in wartime, was disapproved of by government and loathed by Winston Churchill, it was still completed and still released. Think of the punitive action and almost inevitable suffocation that a film and its producers, similarly despised in high places, would face today.

> Three, when we start work on a new idea we must be a year ahead, not only of our competitors, but also of the times. A real film, from idea to universal release, takes a year. Or more.

Now we're really cooking. Here is a professional who is committing himself to excellence. A good film, even a very good film, is not enough. He wants to make a film which is guaranteed to speak for, and indeed to shape, its time. Pressburger is speaking from the height of his powers and he knows it.

Read any description of Powell and Pressburger working together and you'll catch a little of the magic: Michael springing around the room while Emeric sits and nods, sometimes smiles; the discussions of dialogue, the arguments, the electricity and appetite of something being made alive.

Goethe writes in *The Principle of Commitment:* 'Concerning all acts of creation, there is one elementary truth, the ignorance of which kills countless ideas and endless plans, that the moment one definitely commits oneself, then Providence moves too.' Providence moved with Powell and Pressburger and allowed them to be, among other things, remarkably prescient. Not only did they anticipate the concept of the composed film, the potential of the jump cut, the visual projection of intimately psychological realities and the modern interplay of film's medium and its message and the voyeurism of its observers – they could also be frighteningly good at predicting the future. Not long after the 1939 wartime release of *The Spy in Black* – a First World War espionage film where Germans attempt to blow up the British fleet in Scapa Flow – the British ship the *Royal Oak* was attacked in Scapa Flow. Just as the huge impact of the blackout was being experienced by the British public, *Contraband* allowed Powell to explore the dangerous territory of filming in darkness and half light. *Blimp*, apart from showing us how wonderfully colour photography can be used (this was Art Director Alfred Junge's first colour film, a psalm to possibility), also captures perfectly both the promise and the threat in Britain's postwar future. Written during 1942, it clearly points the way that will be taken by the 'fellow of enterprise'[13] decades before our descent into Thatcher's enterprise culture and the society which no longers answers to that name.

In 1940, during a painful delay in the completion of *49th Parallel*, Pressburger wrote to Powell:

> I hope you keep on touching your notebook's leather cover still if you are near to losing your temper. And I hope (and am sure) that finally everything will turn out right and we shall have a very great picture, and we shall show to all who began to doubt our scheme that *they* are the idiots and not we.[14]

Pressburger is writing from within a human relationship about human work that flourishes in an atmosphere of faith. He is writing from a confidence in his team's abilities and, above all, from an enthusiasm for a piece. He is writing from deep within the kind of wonderful, independent and unpredictable mind set which would have caused me, should I have been working in any government department at all, to trust him no further than I could throw a Pugin facade.

> Four, no artist believes in escapism. And we secretly believe that no audience does. We have proved, at any rate, that they will pay to see the truth, for other reasons than her nakedness.

Why is he enthusiastic for the piece? Because he believes the three sentences given above. If I could afford it, I would happily pay to have them reproduced on billboards in every film and television production

Clive takes Edith's sister out on his return from Germany

Aunt Margaret understands immediately

office, every newspaper head office, every publishing house in Britain and beyond. If we studied and applied Pressburger's fourth point, just think what we would save ourselves from.

There would be no more of the exploitative and sexploitative, sub-entertaining sub-entertainment: the semi-satisfying mental and emotional masturbation inflicted upon us by media who would much rather we did not think. The Lottery promises, the gossip, the trivialisation of human nature.

Speaking as a human being, I would rather not be trivialised; life is hard enough without having my dignity stolen, day by day.

Life is hard, I say? Then surely I deserve a break – just an itsy bitsy escape?

Well, actually, no. I deserve better than that. I deserve freedom and the basic assumption that this is my natural state; not a temporary or conditional release, granted by supposed betters. Artists like Pressburger have always offered me this, as articulate equals. They also offer me the truth.

This means that their work will neither present me with something nasty, brutish and probably very long which claims it is realistic because it is unpleasant. Nor will it tidy up human nature so that I will not find it disturbing. They give me the complexity and surreality of truth and they do me the courtesy of assuming that I can understand it, on at least one or two levels. They have the strength of expression and clarity of conception to help me do that. How far I want to take interpretation and analysis is up to me. Many of you will be aware that the British audience has, in many ways, 'grown into' Powell and Pressburger's films. We can accept their darkness, their depth of joy and moral ambivalences now because – as least in part – the film-makers who were influenced by them have broadened our tastes.

Five, at any time, and particularly at the present, the self-respect of all collaborators, from star to prop-man, is sustained, or diminished, by the theme and purpose of the film they are working on. They will fight or intrigue to work on a subject they feel is urgent or contemporary, and fight equally hard to avoid working on a trivial or pointless subject. And we agree with them and want the best workmen with us; and get them. These are the main things we believe in. They have brought us an unbroken record of success and a unique position. Without the one, of course, we should not enjoy the other very long. We are under no illusions. We know we are surrounded by hungry sharks. But you have no idea what fun it is surf-bathing, if you have only paddled, with a nurse holding on to the back of your rompers. We hope you will come on in, the water's fine.

And now we have the only missing element, the one which has been implicit in all the other points: the principle of collaboration founded upon mutual respect. Just as Powell and Pressburger need space and an atmosphere of confidence in which to prosper, so does their production team. And what a team they attracted to the Archers' films. Art director Alfred Junge could be surreal, hyper-real, painterly, suggestive or fastidious – he was always remarkable, winning two Oscars for his work on the visually stunning *Black Narcissus*. Likewise cameraman Jack Cardiff – master of lighting and filters – contributed enormously to the distinctive patina of the Powell and Pressburger canon. Both worked on *Blimp*, to create its strange blend of historical accuracy with a darker, energetic subtext. This was partly achieved by using a characteristically human scale, by concentrating on the detail of costume while allowing settings to have a certain lightness, with scope for the strange significances of a dream. Composer Allan Gray scored *Blimp* with layers of deft pastiche, summarising period as he went, while reiterating Clive's love theme throughout.

I could continue the list with Brian Easdale, who composed for *The Red Shoes* and *Black Narcissus*, or Hein Heckroth, who designed *The Red Shoes* and many other Powell and Pressburger films. Powell and Pressburger weren't afraid to change their team to suit the needs of any given project, but they knew – in their glory days – exactly how to get the best out of their collaborators.

The atmosphere of enthusiasm and concentration from all those present on their sets was legendary, but entirely explicable. As Pressburger points out, people like to be involved with good work – it encourages them to give of their best, and in the process becomes better. Creativity left to its own devices in the right atmosphere will make its own positive cycle, and the enthusiasm and commitment of the makers of a work will be echoed in its recipients. That's how art works. And whenever we forget it, we lose out.

THE MATTER OF LIFE AND DEATH
. . . .

'Now you, alone, will come with me, please.'

Colonel Borg to Clive Candy[15]

It's the perfect introduction for Death – 'Now you, alone, will come with me, please.' That's how Death works and this script knows it. Suddenly events speed, become so plainly irreversible that they are both truly horrifying and truly ridiculous. In the gymnasium at the barracks of the 2nd Uhlans, Clive Candy is prepared to fight a duel. I say 'is prepared' because his own will has nothing to do with his actions; he is being worked upon by a process which may now take him to his extinction.

As an observer, I know that Clive will not die. I have already been introduced to old Clive, post-duel Clive. No self-respecting hero dies in scene 38 of a 118-scene film. But perhaps he will kill his opponent. Perhaps he will suffer that kind of moral death, casually slicing his way out of my affections, leaving me alone with the rest of the script. Because this a moral film, a Powell and Pressburger film, a film with a human centre – you will not become its hero by blowing away bad guys. As we've already mentioned, The Archers' bad guys and their good guys are far too real and complicated for them to get away with something as puerile as that. Powell and Pressburger have already established a tone for their piece which is light and warm, inviting, but there has always been a threat of something darker, winking through. Now here it is again, see?

In the duelling scene, *Blimp* summons up just the preposterous and deadly pace that hurtles in around anything touched with even a scent of death. I recognise the atmosphere. It came for me when I walked to a chapel behind my grandmother's bier and watched four undertakers solemnly wedge themselves between her coffin and the gate. For seconds, or possibly hours, they paddled forward with huge, black feet; crushing in against a box full of meat, or crowding round Mildred Price – my mind was still unable to know which. There seemed to be a lack of respect involved, but I had no idea of what we should be respecting.

Throughout that morning I seemed either to sprint towards the burning of all I had left of my mother's mother – no coming back after that – or to slump into washes of time where I could move through one

Military protocol in the sanatorium

Clive interrogating prisoners of war as Van Zijl looks on

step endlessly, staring at the poor varnish on a coffin, at bad handles and joints. Grandmother was an expert french polisher of the old school, she would never have stood for workmanship like that. But she wanted to be cremated, for there to be no fuss; no visiting her grave with flowers, as if she were an invalid lingering underground. There was no point in making something fancy, just to have it burn.

So Death doesn't march, it races and slips and right now it's whipping Clive Candy up into a jog. We've seen him bundled through rooms of grey men, the quiet type of Blimps, and stumbling into a diplomatic incident. We've seen the proto-Nazi face of politicised Germany and the fatally inflexible logic of her military. We have laughed at the famous Brown Codex governing the conduct of duels. We have been distracted and placated, but now Clive must fight a man he has never met, selected to defend the slighted honour of the German army.

Good Lord, how mediaeval, how un-British. Un-English.

But the English Blimps on offer in Berlin are quite happy to propel Clive into a duel; they even arrange his private affairs to justify it. Before he has noticed he is in love with Edith; they have told him that he must appear to be, for reasons of diplomacy. Clive begins his obsession with Edith by agreeing he will (albeit seem to) fight for her – something he will never do again for himself, even if the lack of her breaks his heart.

In a series of short, neatly satirical scenes we have been brought to the point where two attitudes towards killing collide. An apparently cosy period drama is, once again, wavering on the brink of something quite different, something the MoI and Winston Churchill would not find it in their hearts to smile upon. Pedantic German efficiency and pride face British complacency and gamesmanship. We are looking at a war in miniature. Two unadmirable interest groups have decided they will settle their differences using the living bodies of men – men who have never met, who have no personal enmity, who have simply consented to bleed on behalf of others.

The setting is perfect. The high, bare gymnasium offers no hiding place while its wooden floor makes every footfall batter out like a rifle shot. In civilian dress, the British contingent have a pleasant patina of English amateurishness. But the diplomats accompanying Clive are dressed more like undertakers than amateurs; their movements are assured. They are less openly militaristic than their splendidly uniformed

Uhlan counterparts, but they move into their places with disturbing efficiency. Only Clive, vulnerable in a homely brown suit, seems unaware of the rules of this game. He conducts himself with the innocent confidence of a boy, asks advice, wishes he had his uniform so that he could put up a good show. We are at once protective of him and alarmed by his pre-match levity. Is this how he was in South Africa? Is this how he got his VC? In a film made today, killing might mean so little to Clive because he was either entertainingly psychotic or terminally macho. Here, we realise that he has simply never understood what killing means. We have the chance to realise the importance of understanding this: that killing – even wounding – is no casual thing. This is a film made for grown-ups, a film which is aiming higher than the mythical mass of putty-brained money addicts, or sex- and substance-abusing CJD victims most of the British and American media seem to have fixed forever in their sights.

And talking of madness and abuse, as the businesslike preparations for intentional injury snap into increasingly good order, what do *I* understand? About killing? About my fascination with this section of the film? Why is this scene – and a great many other duelling scenes – so attractive? And how are Powell and Pressburger using my nicely ambivalent, almost guilty attraction?

Why guilty? Because I like the idea of two men fighting over a woman? Or, indeed, anything else? Would I like the idea of two women fighting over a man? A woman fighting a man? I can, for example, clearly recall standing with my grandmother in Wolverhampton's town centre (if you could define such a thing in Wolverhampton) and watching a woman beat a man over his head with her handbag. This sounds quite harmless, but the woman – while screaming loudly – was hitting the man with such frequency and ferocity that blood was already varnishing most of his face. She clearly intended to kill him. Did I like *that?* No, I did not. Do I find boxing and wrestling anything other than repellent? No, I do not. Am I aware that my grandfather's health was permanently damaged by the accumulation of tiny wounds inflicted throughout his boxing career? Yes, I am. I do not approve of fighting when it is bloody, or when it is dressed up as fun. So why the fascination with duellists?

Bear in mind also that I know what the gymnasium sequence could lead to, having been drilled in the techniques of sabre fighting. I fight habitually, though indifferently, with a foil (yes, the obsession has flowered that far) but I have been taught the basic moves for sabre. They are extremely unpleasant.

A foilist practises running people through and avoiding being run through; practises violent but somehow straightforward and oddly lovely acts. At a certain level, I know that I am facing another human being and striving to touch him or her. The touch could once have been fatal, and even now can be quite painful, but it is still a touch.

The sabeur rehearses lopping watermelon slices out of skulls, slashing at the muscle of arms, bluffing and harrying and performing the one particular curving downstroke with an upward flourish designed to open the torso in a flap above the guts. The sabre is a weapon for crippling and disfiguring, for striking down from horseback at Peterloo crowds, for making a dirty kill.

If I didn't know this already, Powell and Pressburger have taken care to warn me. They've told me about scars and had Colonel Borg explain from the codex the procedures to be followed in the case of wounding and drawn blood. Colonel Borg, Swedishly neutral and our MC for this morning, is a worry in himself. He speaks the almost entirely convincing English of an educated European whose understanding may well be imperfect in times of crisis. This morning may become a time of crisis.

And is that the point of attraction? Am I drawn by the idea of a man, about to be pushed to his limits, allowed to flower in that sado-masochistic, voyeuristic, action-film way?

Well, I'm only human.

Yes, I would like to be able to watch Clive in that kind of loving but vivisecting light. (Think of Michael Powell's *Peeping Tom* – he knows what I'm about.) But here I can't indulge my baser motives, because the script makes Clive too unself-aware and too unafraid to play properly into my hands. I am made aware of my appetites, but not allowed to let them cloud my intelligence.

I am, however, also on the brink of falling for the elegance, the eroticism of it all. Because *Blimp* understands how erotic vulnerability can be. Clive is, for example, offered the opportunity of fighting bare-chested. Skin against steel. This would be thoroughly inappropriate for the purposes of our plot, but is still a nice idea. I am allowed a twinge of the nice idea, an impression of the physical substance which is about to be risked. Clive in his shirt and braces, one sleeve torn preparatively away, seems strangely domestic, thoroughly masculine and teasingly close to other sufferings, but I am given no time to linger over him. The rush towards the fight continues.

Once in place, the combatants should take up positions in those tensed, astonishing, seductive poses that are so much a part of fencing. Their legs should flex beautifully to a semi-squat, their arms widening in a kind of ferocious and unrequited embrace. Simultaneously elegant and desperate, they will move at each other erotically, homo-erotically, altogether sexually. This will be Death as sex; its climax guaranteed, although more than averagely messy and damaging.

But I'm not allowed that either. Clive and Theo stretch un-professionally, struggle to prepare themselves without seeming overly keen. There is only a tiny whisper of what might be to come. They stumble across to rosin their feet – a very unromantic detail. And as their seconds take their positions (German and English now both also armed with sabres and identical in their brisk, clinical movements), our duellists are left to face each other in the tiny lifetime of the pause remaining before they must prepare to strike.

Theo Kretschmar-Schuldorff, despite his impressively belligerent name, is not what we expected. Almost frail in his shirt and breeches, he has the eyes of a sensitive, intelligent man. We were told that he has never fought a duel before and now we see why. He is not like the other Germans we have met. He seems embarrassed to be here and guilty for what he may have to do. Once again the film has swung away from preconceptions and stereotypes, away from the general to the human and particular. This is not the theory of a duel, it is the fact. Clive is about to attack a man with the bearing of someone between a schoolteacher and a saint. We are closing on the reality, on the business of professional killing and war. Having been pushed faster and faster towards the fight, we are reined back and forced to stop and to think.

At which point Clive does a terrible thing. He smiles at Theo. *Nothing personal, old chap.* We see Theo's face, a picture of mingled confusion and dismay.

Which is how, wonderfully and simply, with two brief close-ups, *Blimp* opens the relationship between Theo and Clive. Clive is the good-natured child who can smile at the fellow human being he is about to slash at with a sabre, because this seems the friendly thing to do. Theo, born old and cautious, will always be both seduced by the innocence and good Clive represents and repelled by his emotional immaturity and dangerous stupidity.

That one look and its moment of strange human contact makes the duel irrelevant and finally explodes my pleasantly prurient expectations for its coming display. In the terms of this film's personal morality, the duel cannot be shown. The visual beauty of conflict, the adrenaline and release it could offer, will never be provided. *Blimp* will never offer the romance of violence, just as it will never be fooled by the double-talk of politics. We will deal here with individuals and the decisions they must make, based upon standards which must not be influenced by the easy logic of circumstance.

In the terms of Pressburger's plot, the duel is now superfluous. It will not develop character in a useful way, it will provide a false dash of swashbuckling in precisely the wrong place. Because this is a good film with a good script, made by men with a firm and confident understanding of their material, we are shown no more than the opening parries of the duel. Where many other movies would have begun the scene, this one stops it. No one will Uzi anyone into pâté, no stylish music will

With Murdoch at the outbreak of peace

choreograph loose anatomy across walls. We will simply float up and through the gymnasium skylight and out into the snow and the real world where Civil but insensitive Servants have too much power and sensible women have to bear with the lunacy of men.

Outside, waiting in a carriage, 'Baby Face' from the FO doodles in the condensation on the window glass and Edith waits to know the outcome of the duel.

THE ENEMY ALIEN
. . . .

'But at least in 1983 I'll be able to say I was a fellow of enterprise.'
Spud to Clive Candy, Sequence 5.

For some minds, Home can never be safely defined without the help of barriers erected against what it is not. Self-definition comes from a recognition of the enemy and the alien. *Blimp* devotes itself to creating a concept of home, based on personal values, rather than mass hysteria or hatred, but it shows us the dark side of belonging, too. Both the men

Theo, at the concert in the POW camp, refuses Clive's letter

who face each other on the duelling piste will find themselves the enemy and the alien during the course of the film. The woman who waits for them outside will always be just that – outside. But edging in.

To begin with Clive means that I must begin with Roger Livesey; not the first choice for the title role and paid significantly less than the other two leads. Originally, Laurence Olivier was meant to play Clive and he was enthusiastic about his involvement, although the letters from him on his interpretation of the Colonel suggest that it might have been a mildly cataclysmic influence on the film. Olivier's coldly visible intelligence and black edge would have toppled the script into the realms of heavy-handed satire, while his personal dash could have made the romantic plotline either ludicrous or too minor to have any meaning.

Roger Livesey, on the other hand, was and still is ideal. *Blimp* gave him arguably his finest hour as a screen actor, and without him the Clive Candy we know today would be almost unthinkable. Livesey gave the two dimensions of Low's cartoon and the beautiful psychology of Pressburger's script a three-dimensional presence of bluff charm and unassuming grace. Covering forty years of a man's life from gently roguish young officer to blustering Major-General, Livesey lends constants which keep the film from settling into any easy emotional accommodations: physical openness, a consistent gentleness and an almost labrador enthusiasm. And no matter the circumstances, Clive maintains his innocence. 'This childlike stupidity,' Theo announces to a railway carriage full of German POWs, 'is a raft for us in a sea of despair.'[16] Clive represents a type of cleanliness and happiness which can never be fully destroyed and yet which is almost constantly under threat. He is a kind of holy fool, walking the battlegrounds of his century, underestimated and overlooked.

Above all, this sense of softness, humanity and decency is rooted in Livesey's voice. Like non-carcinogenic pipe smoke, like audible cake, like a quintessentially masculine purr, Livesey's voice alone should have made him a star. He did work regularly in theatre and on the screen for something like fifty years. He is charming in *Green Grow the Rushes* and the right actor in the wrong film in the embarrassing *Master of Ballantrae*, but only Powell and Pressburger seem to have really recognised him for the talent he undoubtedly was. He turns up for them in *49th Parallel*, as the lead (a lucky second choice again) in *I Know*

Where I'm Going, and as the camera obscura-wielding doctor-ex-machina to David Niven's pilot in *A Matter of Life and Death.* The Archers always had an eye for class. How much would we have seen of Marius Goring's potential, or of Anton Walbrook's astonishing subtlety and range, without them?

Clive Candy never actually degenerates into one of the puffing* bigots, each with the characteristically baroque walrus moustache, that Low drew, eyeing a preview of *Blimp* with outrage and bewilderment. We can see from the script that some of Clive's more Blimpish mannerisms were toned down or cut during the production. They were rendered unnecessary. Clive's slow drift away from even the very limited realities in which he used to flourish, and his consistent emotional denial, make him a far more sympathetic and far more useful character. He can carry an audience with him and highlight the arrant Blimpery of the British establishment, while representing the kind of delicacy and decency which they have always lacked and which their successors will find new ways to extinguish.

We might also note that Clive Candy is an almost exact inversion of Winston Churchill. Whether this was intentional or not I won't argue

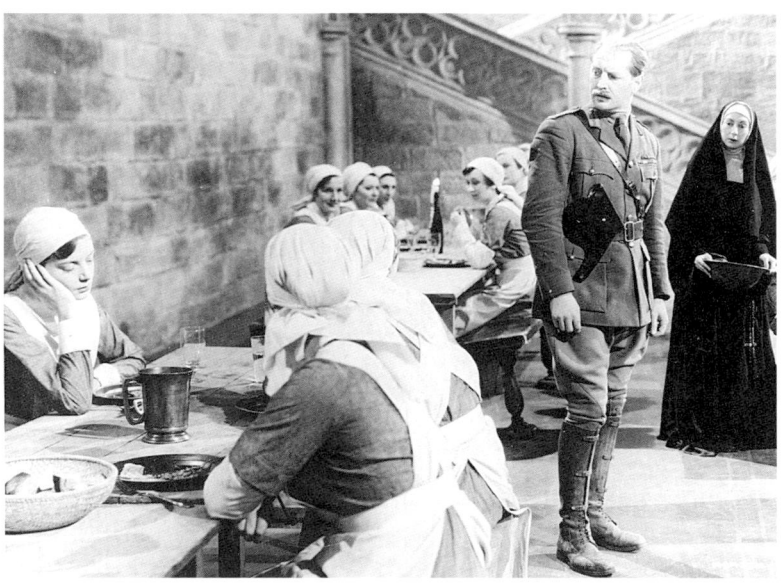

– almost any senior military man whose active life spanned the period between the Boer War and the Second World War would have career landmarks in common with Churchill. It is a matter of record that Churchill loathed *Blimp* with a passion remarkable for a man who was Prime Minister of a country at war and presumably somewhat pressed for time. 'Pray propose to me the measures necessary to stop this foolish production before it gets any further. I am not prepared to allow propaganda detrimental to the morale of the Army, and I am sure the Cabinet will take all necessary action. Who are the people behind it?' rumbles a bullish Churchill at the start of his campaign against the film.[17] This is followed by a steady flurry of bellicose communications, including: 'You and the Secretary of State should bring the matter before the cabinet on Monday when I have no doubt any special authority you may require will be given you',[18] and 'If necessary we must take more powers.'[19]

The premier's attempts to suppress the film and force the Ministry of Information to overstep its powers of censorship greatly aided its box-office appeal. Churchill managed to delay the film's release in America and the Empire, but was warned of the consequences of his

... whom he marries

actions by Brendan Bracken, then Minister of Information. 'As a result of our illegal ban on this wretched film, "Colonel Blimp" has received a wonderful advertisement from the Government. It is now enjoying an extensive run in the suburbs and in all sorts of places there are notices – "see the banned film!"'[20]

How fitting that the Blimps attempting to defeat *Blimp* should be hijacked by their own Blimpery, if it isn't over-egging the pudding to say so. Pressburger would put it better: 'We shall show to all who began to doubt our scheme that *they* are the idiots and not we.'[21]

I must explain that I am no particular friend of Churchill the man who ordered troops to open fire on striking Welsh miners, who made sure that Second World War defensive radar cover did not quite extend to cover Scotland properly, who could have forestalled the hideous destruction and loss of life at Clydebank. I have talked to Clydebank pensioners about the seemingly endless line of bodies in the temporary shelter of a cinema after a wholesale destruction of Home. For me, Churchill will always be the Tory opportunist who edged embarrassingly into newspaper pictures of armed policemen lying in wait for Peter the Painter – that dangerous communist/anarchist Rusky foreign type of chap.

In Clive Candy's career we see some of the script's central messages made clear, and more than enough reasons for Churchill's excess of paranoia.

First, a little more Churchill from his *My Early Life* – a book much beloved in my old school. For, I think, three successive years my class was called upon to study the tale of the great man's daring escape from Boer captivity. (Clive's experience in the Cape was the exact reverse – he *guarded* prisoners.) I have never forgotten the Africaans for 'Who's there?', a phrase Churchill – wily master of languages – used to great effect. I am still surprised that this, and a vague suggestion that modern South Africans had racially as well as sexually segregated toilets, was all I was ever taught about the country. Too many of my classmates were related to Scots who followed our national tradition of emigrating from poverty and injustice at home to shore up systems imposing poverty and injustice upon indigenous populations abroad. The white man's burden.

On 11 October 1899, Churchill tells us, he sailed for the Cape on the *Dunottar Castle* with Sir Redvers Buller. Churchill's pen portrait of him reveals a vintage Blimp. 'Buller was a characteristic British personality. He looked stolid. He said little, and what he said was obscure. He was not the kind of man to explain things, and he never tried to do so.'[22] The very chap to send men into battle. An ideal commander. 'He plodded on from blunder to blunder and from one disaster to another, without losing either the regard of his country or the trust of his troops, to whose feeding as well as his own he paid serious attention.'[23] Churchill, architect of the Gallipoli debacle, would do much the same, gaining favour with the men under his command for preventing them from starving at their posts. Even the basic necessities of life for British troops were long reliant upon the grace and favour of commanding officers.

Although we see that Clive shares many of these stolid qualities, we never see him in a position of active command. His relations with his troops, and even with those of the enemy, hark back to an honour code which has far more to do with his qualities as a man than any genuinely applied military tradition. When Clive questions German troops in front of Major Van Zijl it is obvious that he will get nowhere. He is hardly a student of human nature. Nor is Van Zijl, who is clearly itching to set to work in ways the Geneva Convention would not condone. Scenes where soldiers are tricked into thinking that some of their number have been shot were proposed and, at least partly, filmed. The film today only suggests – perhaps more shockingly – that shameful deeds will soon ensue. We can imagine as we wish.

This sequence is testing for the audience and proved troublesome to the MoI censors. On the page, we see that Bumbling British Niceness gets nothing done, while Nazi Methods are a tempting release of frustration and seem far more effective. But as the film stands, we see that neither course gets any results. One is silly and treats the business of war with no respect, although it treats combatants well. The other is as tempting as evil tends to be. Clive is at home with military personnel: the familiar structure of an army – British, American, German, or Home Guard – allows him to approach a broad spectrum of his fellow men and to grant each of them their dignity. In this respect he is an alien in what should be a guaranteed Home, and might also be a very unBlimpish and effective leader. He is the man, after all, who had suggested that a diplomat might like a taste of the front line. 'It might do him a lot of good!'[24]

Because Clive cannot anticipate the evil in men's actions (for example, he leaves the prisoners at the mercy of Van Zijl) he would be

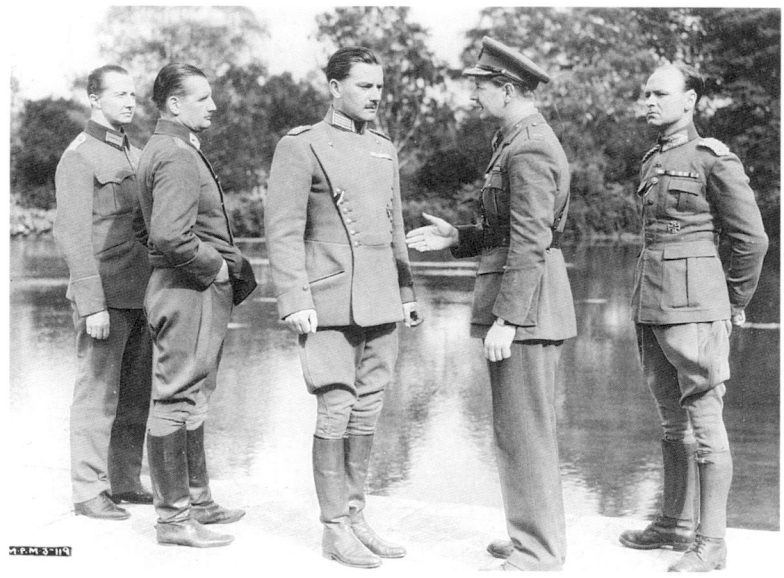

Theo's cold welcome

On his release, Theo faces a table full of blimps

hard pushed to make effective good command decisions. He is, however, much closer to the spirit of Home and What We Are Fighting For than Van Zijl, and, of course, his soul-mate Spud. Powell and Pressburger are suggesting that we have need of a third way.

Although Clive as the young buck we see yodelling opera in the Turkish baths seems full of the braying, sporting energy of a man who sees little difference between war and cricket, we soon learn to see him somewhat differently through the usual Pressburger process of What You See is Less than What You've Got. Clive takes war lightly partly because he is a man of his times, and we soon see how moderate and modern his attitudes are in contrast to the authority figures who surround him. But above all Clive underestimates *himself* and so will never take anything he does too seriously.

I might contrast this with the young Churchill's approach to war as a jolly outing, back on the *Dunottar Castle*. Worried by a signal which seems to suggest that the war will have ended before they arrive and have a chance to join in the fun, a Staff Officer asks Buller his opinion.

'It looks as if it will all be over, sir.'

Thus pressed, the great man answered in the following words: 'I dare say there will be enough left to give us a fight outside Pretoria.'

His military instinct was sure and true. There was quite enough left!

This impressive utterance restored our morale. It was repeated from one to another, and it ran through the ship in a few moments. Every eye was brighter. Every heart felt lighter of its load. The Staff Officers congratulated one another, and the Aides-de Camp skipped for joy.[25]

Brings a lump to the throat, doesn't it? While nicely catching the mentality of Low's Blimp, 'writing' in the *Evening Standard* of 15 January 1943: 'Try to stop fighting and you're bound to make trouble. If you want peace, the only thing is to let everybody fight. Safety first. Events have proved me right.'[26]

We know that, unlike Churchill, Clive will never order artillery to bombard enemy lines just to stir things up a bit if the front line has lacked excitement for a while. Clive will not drag valuable manpower, including his batman, out into no-man's-land and ask them all to risk their lives for little reason beyond the thrill of it. *Blimp* does not show us a glamorous, sporting war. In the trenches here men eat bad food, are beset by torrential rain and navigate in a ruined landscape by the smell of unburied corpses. In the midst of all this Clive and the people close to him stay human. Armstrong – a rare black face in British cinema of the time – is a gentleman and nice to nuns. Clive regards Murdoch, his batman, as a kind of friend and keeps him on after the war to work at his Cadogan Place house. The only request we see Clive use his authority to make is for transport to get him home. The most notable incident in the First World War in which we see him play any part is the moment of the outbreak of peace.

> CLIVE: Murdoch! Do you know what this means?
> MURDOCH: I do, sir. Peace. We can go home. Everybody can go home.
> CLIVE: For me, Murdoch, it means more than that. It means that Right is Might after all. The Germans have shelled hospitals, bombed open towns, sunk neutral ships, used poison gas – and *we won*! Clean fighting, honest soldiering have won! God bless you, Murdoch.[27]

Now this is all fine, patriotic stuff for a film made in the heart of a war, but – I would argue – it is nowhere near as straightforward as it seems. This is the nearest Clive ever gets to stating (or having) his own personal philosophy. This is one of the few points in the film when Home is specifically invoked. We are being told that the aim of all soldiers is to win peace, to return safely to a safe Home, and we certainly trust that Clive believes everything he's saying. But we know he is *wrong*. We have just seen British forces using anything but the methods of honest soldiering on prisoners in their care. Yes, the best man probably has won, but not for the best of reasons. And what of the home Clive returns to? How safe is it and how safe is the peace when evil has already shaken hands with its guardians and good men like Clive are incapable of noticing?

When we move to 1942 and what was then the present day, Clive becomes a figurehead – a little in the manner of Churchill.

His face graces the cover of magazines, yet his influence seems benevolent and unifying, rather than warlike. He finds his niche organising the Home Guard with considerable efficiency. He is finally, professionally, championing the underdog. But we never hear him make a speech. In fact his one broadcast for the BBC – which would have commented adversely on the conduct of the war – is cancelled at the last minute. We can only guess at what he would have said. Frustrated in the studios he shouts at Herbert Marsh, the Acting Director of the BBC.

> CLIVE: I have been asked to describe in this broadcast my views of the cause of the Retreat and its aspects for the future. There they are! I have been serving my country for forty-four years. What was your position before this one, sir? What? A lawyer! *(The Director has murmured 'Lawyer'.)* Well, I was a soldier. And before that, I suppose you were at college. And I was a soldier. And I was a soldier when you were a baby, and before you were born, sir, when you were nothing but a toss-up between a girl's and a boy's name – I was a soldier then! *(He suddenly stops, collects himself, stares at Mr Marsh.)* I'm deeply sorry, sir. I know it's not you. [28]

And if it isn't Mr Marsh, who is it? The government. The MoI. Winston Churchill. The film, in its own way, records the attempts to silence it.

Clive here is not a ranting Blimp, a grand old man, resenting his loss of power to the young. He is a professional who is finally beginning to understand what his life has meant, who was going to offer what he knew to the next generation and who has found himself, for the last time, set aside and undervalued. Spud has won. Home is no longer home. Soon a bomb will flatten Cadogan Place and leave workmen turning through Clive's belongings, the trophies of a collapsing empire.

But what about the third way I mentioned, the course between Clive and Spud? Is there anywhere, apart from in the person of Clive Candy, that our home survives? Characteristically, Powell and Pressburger (classed as an enemy alien throughout the production of *Blimp*) choose to entrust an enemy alien with the key to home. Clive's opposite number in the duel, Theo Kretschmar-Schuldorff – played by Anton Walbrook – knows all about the third way.

Pressburger knew Walbrook from their Ufa days in Germany. At that time Imre Pressburger had changed his name to the Germanic Emerich Pressburger and Walbrook was still Adolf Wohlbruck, a respected screen actor. Half-Jewish, a homosexual and a man of conscience, Walbrook was vehemently anti-Nazi. By 1939 he was establishing himself as an English-speaking actor in Britain. Nevertheless, as Kevin Macdonald points out, he still had a dialogue coach for his English while he worked on *Blimp*, a lady called Edith Williams. It is Edith Hunter, of course, who helps to teach Theo English.

Walbrook had worked on *49th Parallel* with Powell and Pressburger, delivering an astonishing speech against Nazism in his usual precise, controlled but utterly convincing way. He is the only one of *Blimp*'s three leads to be playing in a part written for him, and Theo certainly fits like a glove. Pressburger put all his experience as an outcast, a refugee and a lover of impossible homes into the mouth of Theo, as played by another refugee. Theo is sensitive, cultured, intelligent and irredeemably sad. Walbrook makes him hypnotic, vulnerable, subtle and elegant. His voice is light, measured, still coloured with Walbrook's Austrian accent, and carries a constant undercurrent of emotion. His movements are filled with a tender restraint. If the bluff, dogged Yorkshireman Livesey can stand for Michael Powell, then the quiet, wise Viennese Walbrook stands for Pressburger in an onscreen commemoration of their remarkable friendship.

As in *49th Parallel* and the curtain speech of *The Red Shoes*, Walbrook is entrusted with the keynote monologue for the film. Any other writer would give him the same. Livesey has a voice to die for, but only Walbrook has the delivery to make a credit card statement sound like a declaration of eternally unrequited love. And he isn't given a credit card statement – he is given a kind of prose poem to Home – Pressburger's powerful mixture of nostalgia, hope, fantasy, memory and love. Speaking to the judge who will decide if he can remain in Britain or be sent back to Germany, Theo finally gives up on the refugee's standard repertoire of correct replies. Although he was only in England once before as a prisoner of war, he says, 'The truth about me is that I am a tired old man who came to this country because he is homesick.'[29] The Germany he has left, where his English wife has died and his children have turned against him and joined the Nazis, can no longer be Home. He is now an alien twice over.

He is looking for happiness and a time that cannot return; he is nothing but a longing for something lost. Theo's melancholy is constantly lightened by Clive's fearsome enthusiasm. Clive teases him, calls him 'Prussian stiff-neck' and 'old horse'. He cannot understand why, when Theo is a prisoner, he is too ashamed and confused to shake Clive's hand or even speak to him. He does not understand shame. He has never done anything to be ashamed of. This vulnerability to emotions is part of the third perspective which Theo constantly brings to the film. He feels and then acts upon his feelings. Theo sees Edith for what she is, a beautiful and independent woman; he asks for her hand and gets it.

Theo and his fellow POWs also continue to celebrate what is good and elevated in European culture. Barbara, Clive's new wife, finds the German prisoners confusing.

> BARBARA: I was thinking how odd they are! How queer! For years
> and years they are writing and dreaming wonderful music and
> beautiful poetry and then all of a sudden they start a war, shoot
> innocent hostages, sink undefended ships, bomb and destroy
> whole streets in London, killing little children – and then, dressed
> in the same butcher's uniform, they sit down and listen to
> Mendelssohn and Schubert. There's something horrible about
> that, don't you think so, Clive?
> CLIVE: Hm – mm –[30]

Clive can't answer her, of course. Few people could. Pressburger has presented us with one of the terrible faces of human nature. Taken en masse – and that is how they are taken in times of war – populations seem inexplicable. At times they may seem humane and pleasant, at other times they are the enemy.

Taken as individuals, people are equally complex and contra-dictory, but they can be regarded with forgiveness and compassion much more easily. Compassion is the key to the presentation of all Pressburger's characters. He said of them himself, referring to *The Unholy Passion*, one of his novels, 'As happens so often in life, none of the characters is really bad ... they all have their reasons.'[31]

Blimp shows us that if we underestimate the humanity (the dark and the light) of our enemies we are always wrong and we always risk losing a part of our own human qualities. Thus a surprisingly pleasant German faces Clive in the duel, and thus the First World War German POWs listen to classical music by a Jewish composer and are imbued, like Theo, with the intellectual heritage of Europe. For a moment we, like Clive, are shocked by Theo's rejection of his friendship. Perhaps the enemy really is the enemy, after all. We pause in a dangerous moment. Perhaps Spud's law of the pre-emptive strike should be enforced.

But then Theo softens and is reunited with Clive. An excess of humanity, of human emotion rather than its lack, had prevented him from doing so before. By the time Theo is faced with a dinner table full of the kind but patronising and underinformed Blimps who mean to reorganise Europe after the First World War, we join him in his confusion and dismay. It is clear that a peace built on these terms cannot last, that our home is not safe.

When Theo returns to England in 1942, he brings with him his emotional maturity and his ability to empathise with other human beings. He is the least sociopathic man in *Blimp*. He contains an awareness of man's evil, along with a longing for man's good. His actions have a historical perspective. He has made mistakes in the past – his devotion to military pride, his early tolerance of the Nazis – but he has an ability to learn from errors and not repeat them. He has a lack of intellectual arrogance, a mind forcibly made open by both love and hardship. He can feel love. All these qualities are, I feel, offered to us as the precious parts of humanity without which there will be no home.

Theo longs for a place in the world and for innocence. Clive has too firm a place and a dangerous innocence. Together, the men temper each other. By the end of the film, both of them have lost most of what they have, materially, but each has come much closer to carrying within himself the life, hope and dignity that would be worth fighting for.

Their individual victories are set against a finale which is deeply ambivalent. Clive, Theo and 'Johnny' (Edith's final incarnation) are in the gardens at Cadogan Place. An Emergency Water Supply now occupies the crater where Clive's house used to be. Clive is accepting his defeat at the hands of Spud, smoothing over any trouble his sabotage of Exercise Beer Mug might cause. Clive is making an attempt to pass the baton to the next generation with gallantry. Daydreaming, he remarks to himself that he has not changed, that he is 'hopeless', and yet we see him now as a man who has finally moved towards a kind of definition and strength. His Blimpery has been removed and, just as he is set aside for the final time, he has gained self-knowledge. He now represents values which the 'New Army' may sweep away. In the distance we hear military bands, their music jarringly cheerful. We have a sense of factual victory, but also of dreadful, spiritual loss. There may be a much more bitter struggle to come.

Winston Churchill apparently confronted Anton Walbrook over his involvement with *Blimp*. Walbrook, who was performing in a West End show, found himself suddenly faced by a furious Prime Minister during the interval. Churchill wanted to know what *Blimp* meant, whether Walbrook thought it was supposed to be good propaganda. Walbrook is said to have replied, with characteristic finesse: 'No people in the world other than the English would have had the courage, in the midst of war, to tell the people such unvarnished truth.'[32]

The words of a man who had found a Home he could believe in and was ready to defend it. Bearing in mind that both Pressburger and Walbrook might well have been refused entry to Britain today, I wonder if either of them would say the same of our less than united kingdom now?

Theo being interrogated at the tribunal

LOOKING FOR LERMONTOV
. . . .

'What'll I do if I don't hum?'

Clive to Mrs Candy[33]

Like Lear, Clive Candy is a hero in the tragic, not the heroic, mould. He is taught by time rather than by dramatic actions or experience. His emotional inarticulacy allows him no other course and also denies him the smaller, more romantic fields of combat. Beyond his relations with Theo, Clive has no access to mature love.

In one of the key scenes of the film, Theo and Clive talk in 1942 of their first meeting, forty years before, and of Edith Hunter, Clive's lifelong obsession.

> THEO: Do you remember, Clive, we used to say: 'Our army is fighting for our homes, our women and children.' Now the women are fighting beside the men. The children are trained to shoot. What's left is: the 'home'. But what is 'home' without women and children?
> CLIVE: (*Nods then says suddenly*) You never met my wife. Do you want to see a picture of her?
> THEO: Very much ... (*They both laugh as they stand up*) Do you remember when that was all I could say in English?
> CLIVE: You got further with it then than I ever got.
> THEO: In what respect?
> CLIVE: My dear fellow, don't tell me you didn't know ...
> THEO: What?
> CLIVE: You make me blush!
> THEO: But I don't know what you are talking about.
> CLIVE: Well – I thought it was all over my face when I left Berlin in '02.
> THEO: Don't forget, I never saw your face after you left.
> CLIVE: (*It is a great secret*) I was in love with your wife.
> THEO: (*Slowly*) She never told me ...
> CLIVE: She never knew.
> THEO: But I seem to remember – that last day in Berlin – you seemed genuinely happy ...

CLIVE: Dash it – I didn't know then. But on the train I started to miss her – it was worse on the boat – and by the time I was back in London – well, I'd got it properly. My Aunt Margaret got on the scent straight away, women have a nose for these things. Besides, I did a stupid thing! First night back I took out her sister ...[34]

Here Powell and Pressburger combine the two themes of lost Home and lost love, and perfectly. Here they suddenly reveal a Clive who blushes, who has secrets, who can almost admit that his life has not gone according to plan. This is a wonderful piece of gentle, effective, poignant writing which is acted beautifully.

Theo's opening speech provides his, now inadequate, definition of home. Unlike Clive's statement at the outbreak of peace, this is spoken by a man who has moved beyond propaganda and (mild sexism apart) easy assumptions. In the filmed version, a reference to Germany is cut and, although Theo is clearly referring to his recent experience under Nazi rule, his vision of a ruined future is general. Both Germany and Britain/England have changed beyond recall. He speaks of a place where there are no women and no children. Apart from the personifications of Clive's obsession, *Blimp*'s landscape is singularly lacking in women and children. The damage is done.

But, for once, Clive is determined to make the focus more personal. He has no children and his wife, the image of a woman he could never have, is dead. Delicately, tentatively, he edges into his remarkable confession. Theo and Clive end the next scene together, looking at the portrait of Barbara. In the same way that we are both revolted by and compassionate for James Stewart in *Vertigo* when he dresses his new love to match his dead one, we are stunned by the extent of Clive's emotional wounding. Clive proudly shows Theo the image of a woman with whom he has committed a kind of adultery, lived a kind of waking dream. Theo, who grew old with Edith, does not quite catch the resemblance in Barbara and does not quite know what to say. He responds with the gentle evasions of a friend. We see two ageing men whom time and circumstance have robbed of home, of love and of the newness of romance.

Edith Hunter, an unnamed First World War nurse, Barbara Wynne Candy and Angela 'Johnny' Cannon are all played, of course, by Deborah Kerr. When Wendy Hiller became inconveniently pregnant and Anna Neagle (perish the thought) could not be released, Michael Powell accidentally rediscovered a young, untried actress who had played in excised scenes of *49th Parallel*. Powell's eye for actresses served him well, and Pressburger was also happy to bring Kerr on board.

Kerr's presence is calm but spirited, quietly lovely but unfussy. She allows us to see what Clive sees, to identify completely with his mind-set. When he glimpses her as a nurse, when he finds her in a muted form in Barbara, when he recognises the same, haunting face, we are with him. Murdoch tells us that Clive's sighting of the nurse is not an isolated incident. Angela remarks that she was lucky to get the job as Clive's driver, but Theo (and we) know different. Clive devotes his interior life, little by little, to the pursuit of the impossible, to a search which will make everything he touches seem second-hand.

And, as Theo points out, women are very much connected with home. Each of the women Kerr plays is patient, responsible and thoughtful. They stand aside from a world of male mistakes and excesses. Edith is keenly interested in women's rights, the nurse tends to the victims of a male war, Barbara looks after Clive and is baffled by the atrocities of war, 'Johnny' has taken a male name and does a male job but retains the common sense and decency that her boyfriend Spud has lost.

6 6   Clive learns he has been retired from the army

Women are seen as a stable element, a source of wisdom and compassion. Their move into the male world is bemoaned, not because this wins them a threatening independence, but because it brings them much closer to the heart of corruption and the loss of Home.

To close, I will single out two final quotes from Clive Candy. The first, which heads this chapter, is taken from scene 90 in the script. This is a painfully brief scene between Clive and Barbara – the only one ever to show any kind of domestic life for Clive. The couple sit together in the den Clive has cluttered with trophies he gathered as a kind of displacement activity after losing Edith. (The concept of Empire as a diversion from personal inadequacy is clearly suggested.) Now Clive has the closest wife to Edith he could find. Another trophy. He may well love her, but it is clear that he has no idea of how to pass the time with her. For her part, Barbara speaks to him as if he were a loved child, not a man, correcting his bad habits and asking him not to hum. He can only reply, mystified, 'What'll I do if I don't hum?' He is lost.

The title of this piece is, after all, *The Life and Death of Colonel Blimp*. Clive Candy's underestimation and denial of self leave him with a death in life. He will never know the excitements, the passions, the pains and joys of other men – men like Theo. He will only, now and again, be aware of what he has missed, and will continue to be haunted by a dream woman who stays young and grows more and more active while he ages and fades into impotence.

I am always left with a terrible melancholy after watching *Blimp* – a slight drawback for this project. I am, properly, moved by such a complex and powerful evocation of so much that has come to mean Home to me. Powell and Pressburger's message is still as fresh and powerful as it was, more than fifty years ago. They still give an observer a dreadful desire for Home and a passion for its defence. Because there it all is on screen – the dignity, self-respect, decency, humanity, open-mindedness and altruism that could form Home – just out of reach.

Of course, even before I was born Home was out of reach. Today I can look at the beautiful photographs Jack Cardiff made to hold it, but never touch. Even as the picture was being made, Spud and Van Zijl and the establishment Blimps were making Home unattainable – not an ideal, or a goal, but a simple impossibility. I mention those names together because the 'New Army' and the Blimps are, of course, simply two aspects of the same phenomenon – the force of government, power and establishment which devalues, degrades and then destroys all which it is not. They are the death and the life in death, forced, sometimes quickly and sometimes slowly, on more and more of the inhabitants of this country. Today I might mention names like Portillo, Major and, that great lover of all things Churchillian, Margaret Thatcher. They have made me an alien in my own land.

And they have done it with the mad, rusted iron mind-set of the Blimps. 'We all know how slumps arise – lack of Confidence. The way to deal with Slumps is to be confident that there will be restoration of confidence.'[35] Sound familiar? It shouldn't do. It was written in 1943. But we are still living with it in 1997.

As I have grown older, the condition of my country has deteriorated and my awareness of its decline has increased. This means that *Blimp* moves me more. I am living through a different war, but it is one Powell and Pressburger and Low would recognise, one they foresaw. Naturally, now that I am no longer a child, Clive's personal journey also becomes more understandable and hits the mark increasingly accurately.

I used to think that Clive's obsession with Edith was sad, but noble. I generally found all actresses looked the same and the fact that all

the actresses of importance here *were* the same was a simple convenience. Now when I see the waste of Clive's life, his literal self-effacement and his constant settling for comfortable second bests, I am reminded increasingly of myself. We both go for the safe option – obsession, for example, is much safer than love. We are both too taken up in our work to live entirely normally. We both seem to take a perverse pride in being overlooked. I am afraid, like many people, of missing my own life. I worry, like many people, that the part of a literal home which resides in others – in one other person – will never be reached.

Which is where my second, and last, quote comes in. 'Besides, I did a stupid thing! First night back I took out her sister.' Remember? Clive took out Edith's sister because he hoped she might be like her and he made the sad discovery that sometimes *almost* is worse than *not at all*. He spent an evening willing someone into someone else, which is both pointless and unfair but also very human.

I had forgotten the scene when I first watched *Blimp* again for this book. In the intervening years, I had inadvertently made a new point of identification with Clive. I had spent an evening with a very pleasant man who had no way of knowing that I'd met him because he looked very slightly like someone else – an angle of bone here, a smile there. My imagination would not let me appreciate him for himself, which was both pointless and unfair.

Years ago I made part of Home out of movies – movies filled with strolling, suited, quietly elegant men. The collars and cuffs, the braces and soft hats, still haunt me, like that one slow picture of Lermontov. My benchmark for masculinity is decades out of date. Equally, my expectations of happiness, of a Home peopled by men and women who have room to breathe, to form lives of dignity and love, are equally anachronistic. The insoluble ache which seems to be an essential part of Home is in danger of degenerating into simple, self-destructive grief.

I am certain that Powell and Pressburger and *The Life and Death of Colonel Blimp* are firmly a part of the Home I carry with me – of that need for more and better which I think is part of being alive. Although they can bring me close to despair when I think of all they represent and how much of it is now lost, they also provide encouragement, constructive anger and hope, as good art should. When I find myself walking through Chinatown and feel a familiar cold, I am not lonely and I am not completely undefined.

NOTES

. . . .

1 Kevin Macdonald, *Emeric Pressburger: The Life and Death of a Screenwriter* (London: Faber and Faber, 1994), p. 383.

2 *The Life and Death of Colonel Blimp* (script), ed. Ian Christie (London: Faber and Faber, 1994), scene 15. All subsequent references to the script are from this edition.

3 Ibid., p. 31.

4 Ibid., scene 2.

5 Ibid.

6 Ibid., scene 15.

7 Ibid., p. 37.

8 Ibid., p. 76.

9 Ibid., p. 16.

10 Ibid., pp. 16–17.

11 Macdonald, *The Life and Death of a Screenwriter*, p. 86.

12 Ibid., p. 156.

13 *The Life and Death of Colonel Blimp* (script), scene 15.

14 Macdonald, *The Life and Death of a Screenwriter*, p. 178.

15 *The Life and Death of Colonel Blimp* (script), scene 38.

16 Ibid., scene 89.

17 Ibid., p. 44. Letter from Churchill to Minister of Information, 10 September 1942.

18 Ibid., p. 49. Letter from Churchill to Minister of Information, 11 July 1943.

19 Ibid., p. 50. Letter from Churchill to Minister of Information, 25 July 1943.

20 Ibid., p. 50. MoI memorandum, 5 August 1943.

21 Macdonald, *The Life and Death of a Screenwriter*, p. 178.

22 Winston Churchill, *My Early Life*, (London: Mandarin, 1990), p. 248.

23 Ibid.

24 *The Life and Death of Colonel Blimp* (script), scene 23.

25 Churchill, *My Early Life*, p. 251.

26 *The Life and Death of Colonel Blimp* (script), pp. 303–4. David Low, *Evening Standard*, 15 January 1943.

27 Ibid., scene 69.

28 Ibid., scene 100.

29 Ibid., scene 93.

30 Ibid., scene 76.

31 Macdonald, *The Life and Death of a Screenwriter*, p. 389.

32 Ibid., p. 224.

33 *The Life and Death of Colonel Blimp* (script), scene 90.

34 Ibid., scene 94.

35 Ibid., p. 305. David Low, *Evening Standard*, 15 January 1943.

CREDITS

· ·

The Life and Death of Colonel Blimp

UK
1943
Production company
A Production of the
Archers
UK trade show
8 June 1943
UK release
26 July 1943
US release
4 May 1945
Distributor
General Film Distributors
US Distributors
United Artists
Producers
Michael Powell,
Emeric Pressburger
Management
Sydney S. Streeter,
Alec Saville
Archers secretary
Joan Page
Assistant producer
Richard Vernon
Floor manager
Arthur Lawson
Directors
Michael Powell,
Emeric Pressburger
Assistant directors
Ken Horne,
Tom Payne
Screenplay
Michael Powell,
Emeric Pressburger;
with acknowledgment to
David Low, 'creator of the
immortal Colonel'
**Photography
(Technicolor)**
Georges Perinal
Chief electrician
Bill Wall
**Music/
music arrangement**
Allan Gray

Conductor
Charles Williams
Editor
John Seabourne
Assistant editors
Thelma Myers,
Peter Seabourne
Production design
Alfred Junge
Costume design
Joseph Bato
Costumes executed
Matilda Etches
Make-up
George Blackler,
Dorrie Hamilton
Military adviser
Lt. General Sir Douglas
Brownrigg
Period advisers
E.F.E. Schoen,
Dr C. Beard
Sound
C.C. Stevens,
Desmond Dew
**Chief of colour control
department**
Natalie Kalmus
Technicolor cameramen
Geoffrey Unsworth,
Jack Cardiff,
Harold Haysom
Process shots
W. Percy Day
[Production runner
Tom White
Production manager
Roger Cherrill]

163 minutes
1470 feet (trade show
footage)

James McKechnie
Spud Wilson
Neville Mapp
Stuffy Graves

Vincent Holman
Club porter (1942)
Roger Livesey
Clive Candy
David Hutcheson
'Hoppy' Hopwell
Spencer Trevor
Period Blimp
Roland Culver
Colonel T.H. Betteridge
James Knight
Club porter (1902)
Deborah Kerr
Edith Hunter
Dennis Arundell
Café orchestra leader
David Ward
Kaunitz
Jan van Loewen
Indignant citizen
Valentine Dyall
Von Schonborn
Carl Jaffe
Von Reumann
Albert Lieven
Von Ritter
Eric Maturin
Colonel Goodhead
Frith Banbury
'Baby-face' Fitzroy
Robert Harris
Embassy secretary
Arthur Wontner
Embassy counsellor
Count Zichy
Colonel Borg
Anton Walbrook
Theo Kretschmar-Schuldorff
Jane Millican
Nurse Erna
Ursula Jeans
Frau von Kalteneck
Phyllis Morris
Pebble
Muriel Aked
Aunt Margaret Hamilton
John Laurie
John Montgomery Murdoch

Reginald Tate
Van Zijl
Captain W.H. Barrett,
US Army
The Texan
Corporal Thomas
Palmer, US Army
The sergeant
Yvonne Andree
The nun
Marjorie Gresley
The matron
Deborah Kerr
Barbara Wynne
Felix Aylmer
The Bishop
Helen Debroy
Mrs Wynne
Norman Pierce
Mr Wynne

Harry Welchman
Major John E. Davis
A.E. Matthews
President of tribunal
Deborah Kerr
Angela 'Johnny' Cannon
Edward Cooper
BBC official
Joan Swinstead
Secretary
Diana Marshall
Sibyl
Wally Patch
Sergeant with debris-clearing unit
George Woodbridge
Man with debris-clearing unit
Ferdy Mayne
Prussian student
John Boxer
A soldier

Ian Fleming
Major Plumley
Peter Noble
Prisoner of war
John Varley
Patrick Macnee

US title:
Colonel Blimp

Credits checked by
Markku Salmi.

The print of *The Life and Death of Colonel Blimp* was produced for the 360 Classic Feature Films project from original Technicolor material fully restored by the National Film and Television Archive.

ALSO PUBLISHED

If you would like further information about future BFI Film Classics or about other books on film, media and popular culture from BFI Publishing, please write to:

BFI Film Classics
British Film Institute
21 Stephen Street
London
W1P 2LN

THE BIG SLEEP

....

David Thomson

BRIDE OF FRANKENSTEIN

· · · · · · · · · · · · · · · · · · ·

Alberto Manguel

LES ENFANTS DU PARADIS

·····················

Jill Forbes

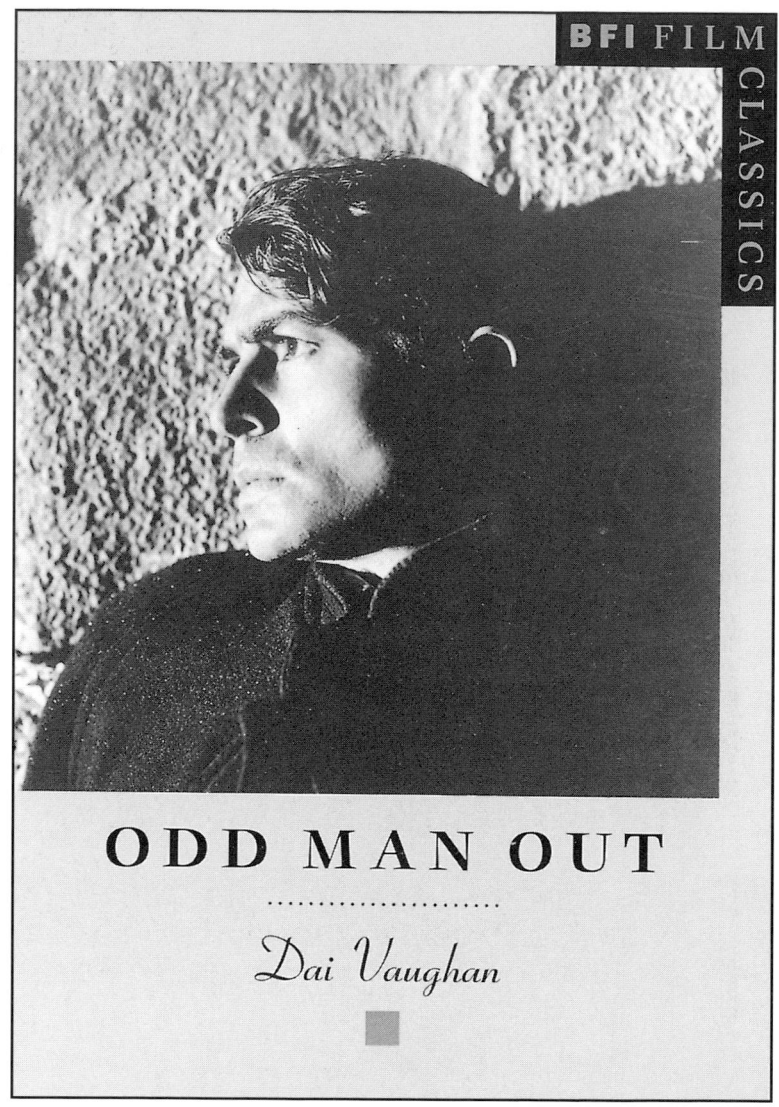

BFI FILM CLASSICS

ODD MAN OUT

....

Dai Vaughan

BFI FILM
CLASSICS

WENT THE DAY WELL?

....

Penelope Houston

"*The strength of the best Anglo-Saxon tradition of film criticism - finely crafted
and intellectually rigorous - is discernable on each page*"
THE TIMES

Each book in the BFI Film Classics series honours a great film from the history of world cinema. With four new titles published each spring and autumn, the series will rapidly build into a collection representing some of the best writing on film. Forthcoming titles include *Citizen Kane* by Laura Mulvey, *The Big Heat* by Colin McArthur, *Brief Encounter* by Richard Dyer and *L'Atalante* by Marina Warner.

If you would like to receive further information about future BFI Film Classics or about other books on film, media and popular culture from BFI Publishing, please fill in your name and address below and return the card to the BFI.

No stamp is needed if posted in the United Kingdom, Channel Islands, or Isle of Man.

NAME

ADDRESS

POSTCODE

BFI Publishing
21 Stephen Street
FREEPOST 7
LONDON
W1E 4AN